George Fisher Daniels

The Huguenots in the Nipmuck Country

Oxford Prior to 1713

George Fisher Daniels

The Huguenots in the Nipmuck Country
Oxford Prior to 1713

ISBN/EAN: 9783337235871

Printed in Europe, USA, Canada, Australia, Japan

Cover: Foto ©Thomas Meinert / pixelio.de

More available books at **www.hansebooks.com**

THE

HUGUENOTS

IN THE

NIPMUCK COUNTRY

OR

Oxford Prior to 1713

BY GEORGE F. DANIELS

WITH AN INTRODUCTION BY

OLIVER WENDELL HOLMES

Plantations are amongst ancient, primitive, and heroical works.— BACON

BOSTON

ESTES & LAURIAT

1880

PREFACE.

EVERY fact relating to the Huguenots, however slight, has a notable interest. It has been well said that they gave a lustre and a glory to every place and to every thing they touched. The history, therefore, of their sojourn in the "Nipmuck Country," while it is the first chapter in the history of the Town of Oxford, is in itself, independently, a story which will be appreciated by many in our country who have no special interest in the locality.

It has been the design in this memoir to bring together all the facts referring to the Oxford Colonies, from every available source, and to arrange them, so far as possible, in such a manner as might best set forth the course of events, adding only such legitimate inferences and comments as would seem to be demanded to complete the narrative.

Special thanks are here tendered to Rev. Chas. W. Baird, D. D., of Rye, N. Y., who has given very essential aid in the preparation of this volume, by the contribution of important facts, and of original documents, both English and French in translation, these having been collected by him during his extensive researches for materials for his "*History of the Huguenot Emigration to America*," soon to be published.

If the result of the publication of this little volume shall be to awaken in the people of Oxford a deeper interest in the history of the town, and to move them to take action for the continuance of the work of its preparation by a more competent hand, the writer will feel that his labors have not been in vain.

CONTENTS.

CHAPTER I.

CHAPTER II.

CHAPTER III.

CHAPTER XI.

INTRODUCTORY.

(OLIVER WENDELL HOLMES,

To GEORGE F. DANIELS.)

My Dear Sir : —

I have read carefully, and with great interest, but not critically, the manuscript you sent me. I say not critically, because it would be a work of much labor to follow you through your long and pains-taking investigations, and this I cannot pretend to have done. I am sure, however, that your memoir is a true labor of love, performed conscientiously, for its own sake, and a valuable contribution to our local history.

Of all my father's historical studies, none ever interested me so much as his "Memoir of the French Protestants who settled at Oxford, in Massachusetts, A. D. MDCLXXXVI." All the circumstances connected with that second Colony of Pilgrim Fathers are such as to invest it with singular attractions for the student of history, the antiquary, the genealogist. It carries us back to the memories of the Massacre of Saint Bartholomew, to the generous Edict of Nantes and the gallant soldier-king who issued it; to the days of the Grand Monarque, and the cruel Act of Revocation which drove into exile hundreds of thousands of the best subjects of France — among them the little band which was planted in our Massachusetts half tamed wilderness. It leads the explorer who loves to linger around the places consecrated by human enterprise, efforts, trials, triumphs, sufferings, to localities still marked with the fading traces of the strangers who there found a refuge for a few brief years, and then wandered forth to know their homes no more. It tells the lover of family history where the un-English names which he is constantly meeting with — Bowdoin, Faneuil, Sigourney — found their origin, and under what skies was moulded the type of lineaments, unlike those of Anglo-Saxon parentage, which he finds among certain of his acquaintance, and it may be in his own family or himself.

And what romance can be fuller of interest
than the story of this hunted handful of Protestants leaving, some of them at an hour's warning,
all that was dear to them, and voluntarily
wrecking themselves, as it were, on this shore,
where the savage and the wolf were waiting
ready to dispute possession with the feeble
intruders? They came with their trained skill
to a region where trees were to be felled, wild
beasts to be slain, the soil to be subdued to
furnish them bread, the whole fabric of social
order established under new conditions. They
came from the sunny skies of France to the
capricious climate where the summers were fierce
and the winters terrible with winds and snows.
They left the polished amenities of an old civilization, for the homely ways of rude settlers of
another race and language. Their lips, which
had shaped themselves to the harmonies of a
refined language, — which had been used to speaking such names as Rochefort and Beauvoir and
Angoulême, — had to distort themselves into the
utterance of words like Manchaug and Wabquasset

and Chaubunagungamaug. The short and simple annals of this brave and gentle company of emigrants are full of trials and troubles, and ended with a bloody catastrophe. The Indians to whom "*rome* was sold without order and measure" were complained of as getting "so furious with drunkness that they fought like bears." They fell upon, and dangerously if not fatally wounded one of the preachers sent among them. At length the massacre of four of a family of five persons by the savages, broke up the settlement, and though some few of the original colonists returned for a season, the place was soon finally deserted.

My father visited the site of the little colony in 1819 and 1825. He traced the lines of the fort, and was "regaled with the perfumes of the shrubbery and the grapes then hanging in clusters on the vines planted by the Huguenots above a century before." I visited the place between twenty and thirty years ago, and found many traces of the old settlement. After Plymouth; I do not think there is any locality in New England more interesting. This little band of French families, transported from the shore of the Bay of Biscay to the wilds of our New England interior, reminds me of the isolated group of magnolias which we find surrounded by the ordinary forest trees in our Massachusetts town of Manchester. It is a surprise to meet with them, and we wonder how they came there, but they glorify the scenery with their tropical flowers, and sweeten it with their fragrance. Such a pleasing surprise is the effect of coming upon this small and transitory abiding-place of the men and women who left their beloved and beautiful land for the sake of their religion. The lines of their fort may become obliterated, "the perfumes of the shrubbery" may no longer be perceived, but the ground they hallowed by their footsteps is sacred, and the air around their old Oxford home is sweet with their memory.

BOSTON, June, 1879.

"The savage arrow scathed them, and dark clouds
Involv'd their infant Zion, yet they bore
Toil and affliction with unwavering eye
Fixed on the heavens, and firm in hope sublime
Sank to their last repose.   Full many a son
Among the noblest of our land looks back
Through Time's long vista, and exulting claims
These as his Sires." — L. H. S., Holmes' Mem. 83.

CHAPTER I.

THE Town of Oxford has its site near the middle of a large territory lying mainly in the southern central part of Massachusetts, known at the time of the settlement of Boston, in 1630, as the " Nipmuck Country." Its bounds were very indefinite, but it extended from the vicinity of Natick, westerly to the Connecticut river, and from the vicinity of Worcester, southerly some twenty-five or thirty miles, down the Quinebaug valley, into what is now Connecticut.

The first mention we have in history of this locality, occurs in the record of an excursion of John Winthrop and a few friends, in 1632. Wishing to spy out this region, then almost unknown, they ascended the Charles river so far, that from a high position they overlooked, as they reported, the whole Nipmuck Country, and " saw a very high hill, due west." Three years later a company of sixty settlers from

2

Watertown, being desirous of possessing more land than that place could afford them, took their way over the Indian trails westward, bound for the rich intervals of the Connecticut valley, and "seized a brave piece of meadow" at Wethersfield. Doubtless they passed near the site of this village, and probably were the first white men who trod the soil of this region. At that time the westerly part of this tract was wild hunting ground, and the eastern portion was quite thinly inhabited by the Nipmuck Indians in scattered villages, their numbers having been greatly reduced by recent wars with western tribes, and by fatal disease.[1]

· The name "Nipmuck," or " Nipnet," which signifies "fresh water," was given to all the dwellers upon this large inland tract, to distinguish them from the more numerous and powerful tribes which lived upon the sea coast.[2]   They were an inferior people, who appear to have owed some fealty to the Pokanokets.[3]   Miss Larned, in her History of

[1] Brigham's Centennial Add., Grafton, 1835.

[2] This name, in its original signification, was applied to other tribes in New England, but it came to have a special application to the inhabitants of this central Massachusetts region. Different branches of this tribe assumed the names of the particular localities in which they lived.

[3] Palfrey Hist. New Eng., 1. 24.

Windham County, well describes them thus:

"They were subject clans, of little spirit or distinctive character. Their number was small. A few families occupied the favorable localities, while large sections were left vacant and desolate. Their dwellings were poor, their weapons and utensils rude and scanty. They raised corn and beans, and wove mats and baskets. Their lives were chiefly spent in hunting, fishing and idling."

They did not exhibit the enterprise and intelligence of the neighboring tribes, but seemed more peaceful and inclined to assimilate with the whites as they came to have intercourse with them; and, as did other tribes in the Colony, early showed a disposition to become civilized and to have the institutions of religion established among them.

The General Court of Massachusetts, wishing to meet these wants, passed an order Nov. 19th, 1644, inaugurating measures looking toward their Christianization and improvement,[1] thus becoming, as Palfrey says, "the first missionary society in the history of Protestant Christendom."[2] In 1646, John Eliot, known as the "Apostle to the Indians," having been for fourteen years teacher of the Roxbury Church, and through the instrumentality of a native

---

[1] Palfrey, II. 188.   [2] Ibid., 189.

servant, having learned the rudiments of the Indian
language, began his labors in Nonantum, a part of
Newton.[1] In 1651 he removed the headquarters of
his operations to Natick, and while still retaining
his pastorate at Roxbury, for nearly twenty-five
years, until interrupted by Philip's war, he and his
co-laborers traveled, preached, taught and advised in
matters civil and religious, establishing schools,
founding churches, and installing native teachers
and pastors among many tribes in the province,
including this far off and humble people of the
Nipmuck Country.[2]

[1] Palfrey, II. 190.

[2] "The "Society for the Propagation of the Gospel in New
England," whose headquarters were in London, entered upon
its work with considerable efficiency. So far as practicable it
co-operated with Eliot, who was encouraged in his labors by
an annual "honorarium" paid by the society, he receiving at
first fifteen pounds, then twenty, [Gookin.] and afterward fifty.
[Hazard, II. 378.] He did not, however, always act harmo-
niously with the commissioners of the Society, but differed with
them as to ways and means, and thus incurred the censure of
its managers, who characterized his proceedings as "turbulent
and clamorous," but still retained his services and ordered his
salary to be increased. [Hazard, II. 332.] These commissioners
selected native young men to be educated at Cambridge as
teachers, and had authority from the Society to erect there a
building "thirty feet in length and twenty feet in width," for

To a considerable extent success attended their labors, especially in those villages which were near the English settlements on the eastern coast. Seven communities were established from Hassanamesit — now Grafton — eastward, and were called "praying towns," and later, from that place to Wabquasset, now Woodstock, were established five others, which were called "new praying towns." [1]

native pupils. They encouraged education by giving bounties, they printed catechisms in the native language, and furnished books for teachers. [Palfrey, II. 333.] In 1658 Eliot's native teachers were paid ten pounds each, and he received two pounds for Bibles, spectacles and primers for the natives. The outlay of the Society in this, the eighth year of its operations, was five hundred and twenty pounds, chiefly in salaries to teachers, and the sustaining of pupils in the schools at Cambridge. [Ibid.] Mr. Eliot's efforts were put forth for the civilization as well as the Christianization of the people. He encouraged the building of frame houses, and the making of homes for separate families, the planting of gardens and orchards, the raising and utilizing of flax and hemp, and at Natick, under his direction, a bridge eighty feet long was built across the river, and a hall fifty by twenty-five feet was erected for public worship. [Ibid. II. 336, 337.]

[1] The seven "old praying towns" were these: — Natick, Pakemitt, now Stoughton, — Ockoocangansett, now Marlborough, — Wamesitt, now Lowell, — Hassanamesit, now Grafton,— Nashobah, now Littleton, — Magunkook, now Hopkin-

Hassanamesit became the centre of influence in this circle of praying communities. It was the dwelling place of Wattascompanum, chief ruler of the tribe, a professed convert to Christianity, who was an efficient aid to the English magistrate in managing the civil affairs of the Indians, and who exerted a controlling influence among his own people. A flourishing school was established there, from which native teachers went out to neighboring villages, [1] the forms of civil government were to some extent adopted, the Bible in their native language was within reach of all, and was taught them by native teachers in every village, and notwithstanding many things which remained unpromising, Eliot and his companion in labor, Daniel Gookin, [2] who from 1656 had been "betrusted and employed for the civil government and conduct of the Indians in Massachusetts Colony," were encouraged to believe that

ton. Gookin, in his account of a visit with Eliot to the Nipmucks in 1674, gives the names of the "new praying towns," beginning with Manchaug, now Oxford, twelve families, — Chaubunagungamaug, now Webster, five miles southerly, nine families, — Maanexit on the Quinebaug river, four or five miles further south, — Quantisset, now Thompson Hill and Wabquasset, now Woodstock.

[1] Brigham's Add.
[2] Palfrey, II. 338.

these people were to become Christianized, and thus made the friends and helpers of the settlers who were to come among them.

Yet, underneath all this fair and promising exterior there lay the peculiar Indian character. The test came when " Philip of Pokanoket" rallied all his allies to make his grand assault upon the English colonies in 1675. Then those instincts which have shown themselves in most of the native tribes of our country, appeared in the Nipmucks in all their malignity, and when once aroused, these apparently quiet and inoffensive men did not shrink from the commission of deeds most shocking and barbarous. There were, indeed, exceptions, for in the new praying towns a few, and in the old praying towns many, adhered to their alliance with the English ; but the more remote branches of the tribe from Ilassanamesit westward, to use the language of Gookin, "being raw, and lately initiated in the Christian profession, most of them fell off from the English and joined the enemy." [1] Apparently their alliance with the settlers had been founded on a basis of justice, and their better judgment doubtless

---

[1] " The Wabquassets did not join Philip, but fled southward and placed themselves under the protection of Uncas, at Mohegan." Miss Larned, Hist. Wind. Co., I. 10.

would have held them firmly to the whites as their
true friends, but Philip plied them with argument
and solicitation, possibly also urging his claims to
their support as subjects, until they yielded. In
the words of Palfrey,—

" A taste for havoc was established between heathen
Wampanoag and half converted Nipmuck. Without
provocation, and without warning, they gave full sway
to the inhuman passions of their savage nature, and
broke into a wild riot of pillage, arson and massacre."

During that disastrous time, the summer, autumn
and winter of 1675, they pursued their deadly work
among the colonists, not only of this region but also
of the Connecticut valley, and throughout the interior
of the state, ruin and disaster prevailed. Mendon,
Lancaster, Brookfield and Worcester, the only settlements in this county, were burned, and more or less
of savage cruelty attended their destruction. Capt.
Wheeler, with twenty men sent from headquarters as
an escort to Mr. Edward Hutchinson, who came on a
peaceful errand to the Nipmucks, was drawn by them
into an ambush near Brookfield, on the 2d of August
1675, and he and three others were wounded,
and eight men killed.[1]   One day previous to this
attack, Philip being hard pressed by his pursuers,

1 Palfrey, III. 159.

came up from his refuge near the coast, and with his
forty attendants was received and sheltered here.[1]
Wattascompanum became one of Philip's most pliant
aids, and was very efficient in seducing the praying
Indians from their fidelity.[2] Gookin says, he was "a
prudent, and I believe a pious man, and had given
good demonstration of it for many years. This
man yielded to the enemy's arguments, and by his
example drew most of the rest." Matoonas, another
chief, also gave the English much trouble. He made
some pretence to religion, and in 1674 was appointed
constable at Pakachoag.[3] But he had a grudge
against the whites because of the execution of his
son for murder in 1671, and when the war broke out
he was ripe for revenge. He became one of the
foremost of the assailants, led in their dances, and
in the attack on Mendon was at their head, and
killed four or five persons himself. A writer of the
time called him "an old, malicious villain."[4]

Increase Mather says,

"Matoonas was the first Indian that treacherously shed English blood in the Massachusetts colony. He some years before
pretended to something of religion, being a professor in general

[1] Palfrey, III. 159.   [2] Ibid. III. 220.

[3] Gookin speaks of him as "that grave and sober Indian."

[4] Drake, Am. Ind.

(though never baptized nor of the in-churched Indians) that he might more covertly manage the hellish designs of revenge that were harbored in his devilish heart." [1]

"James the printer," a promising young man of Hassanamesit, joined Philip, and led a company of warriors against the colonists. [2]

"Frequently the marauders in the Nipmuck Coun-

---

[1] Drake, App.

[2] "James the Printer" seems to have been one of the most interesting Indian characters mentioned in the accounts of those early times. When a child he was taken into the Indian school at Cambridge, and was afterward apprenticed—probably to Mr. Green—for sixteen years, to learn the art of printing, but ran away before his time expired. He was Eliot's most valuable assistant in printing the Indian Bible. In 1683 this worthy man wrote thus to a friend in London, in reference to a revised edition of this book, — "I desire to see it done before I die, and I am so deep in years that I cannot expect to live long; besides, we have but one man, viz., the Indian printer, that is able to compose the sheets and correct the press with understanding."

James was sometime teacher, both at Hassanamesit and Chaubunagungamaug, and worked at printing after the war, and, in company with Mr. Green, printed the Indian Psalter in 1709.

"Printer" became the surname of the family, and his reputed descendants have lived in Grafton, until within a very few years past. Pierce, Hist. Grafton.

try were recognized as professors of Christianity, nor
in that region was it found that any community, or
any considerable number of natives could be relied
on as allies." [1]

Yet, though the Nipmucks acted a prominent part in
this tragedy, they did not receive the retribution which
their deeds would have seemed to demand. We find
recorded no war-like movement against them as a
tribe, except the occasional coming among them of
small foraging parties for corn and swine, and the
expedition of Capt. Gorham, with one hundred men,
from Plymouth, in October, 1675, who burned their
corn-fields and a few wigwams and mats. [2] In June,
1676, Maj. Talcott and four hundred and fifty men,
English and Indians, were marching from Norwich to
join the Massachusetts troops at Brookfield, on their
way to the Connecticut valley. At Wabquasset they
destroyed a deserted fort and the growing corn, and
at Chaubunagungamaug killed and captured fifty-two
Indians. [3]

But rigid civil restraint was resorted to. The
authorities issued special orders, requiring the
tribe to come together in five places which were
named, and there build wigwams in compact settlements, and not to go more than a mile away from

---

[1] Palfrey, III. 199.   [2] Gookin.   [3] Conn. Rec., II. 453.

of his captain, Annawon, which occurred August
28th, virtually ended the contest.[1]

To the Nipmucks the results of this war were
disastrous in the extreme. The execution of so many
of their prominent men, added to other losses incident to such a struggle, had the effect completely to
prostrate them, and only a feeble and spiritless rem-
nant was found here when the English commenced
negotiations with them preparatory to a settlement.[2]

"This war was very disastrous to the labors of Mr. Eliot, and
almost entirely suspended them. The irritation against the
Indians was very great, and jealousy and distrust of his
converts were everywhere rife, and the rage of the people was
violent and alarming. Mr. Gookin and Mr. Eliot incurred much
abuse."[3]

The indignation against the natives, on account of
their faithlessness, was general and deep-seated among
the English. Eliot, Gookin, and Thomas Danforth
pleaded alone in their behalf before the government,
and the last two were threatened with death on this

[1] Palfrey, III. 206.
[2] "The Nipmucks found themselves almost annihilated."
Miss Larned, I. 11.
[3] Morton's N. E. Mem., 391.—"Six years after the close of
the war, Eliot could claim but four towns in the state." One of
these was Chaubenagungamaug.—Drake, 179.

account.[1]   But it would seem that in the excitement, in the case of Wattascompanum at least, great injustice was done.

Drake says, " Some of the proceedings against this man have of late been brought to light.   His case is one of most melancholy interest, and his fate will be deeply regretted ; inasmuch as the proof against him, so far as we can discover, would not at any other time be deemed worthy of a moment's consideration. The younger Eliot pleaded earnestly for him that he might even have a new trial, but without avail."

---

[1] Mass. Arch., XXX. 193.

CHAPTER II.

THE first movement toward a settlement in the Nipmuck Country after the close of the war, was the petition of Mr. Hugh Campbell, a Scotch merchant of Boston, in February, 1680, for land for a colony. The General Court granted his petition, but we have nothing to show that a settlement was begun. The answer of the Court to Mr. Campbell's petition is as follows : —

"This Court judgeth it meete to allow to the petitioner, on behalfe of such as may on that account transport themselues hither, such accomodation to their number in the Nepmug country as it will affoord, prouided they come w'thin two yeares next after this grant." [1]

From the index to this record we learn that this grant was made in behalf of a company of Scotch emigrants who were purposing to settle in Massachusetts.

At about the same, time two leading men in the

---

[1] Mass. Col. Rec., V. 263.

Province, William Stoughton and Joseph Dudley, were also contemplating a settlement in this region. The venerable Eliot — Dudley's pastor — who by his repeated visits here had become familiar with its resources, and his co-laborer and friend Gookin, who also knew both people and country well, doubtless encouraged the plan, as their strong desire was that the institutions of civilization and religion might be re-established among the Indians, who were in a sense their wards, and whose welfare would be largely affected by such influences as a colony of settlers might bring.

In proceeding with their plan, the first point with these gentlemen was to inquire into the matter of the ownership of the lands they proposed to occupy, and the rights of the Indians in them. On this subject they petitioned the General Court.

In answer to this motion and petition the Court replied, May 11th, 1681, as follows :

"The Court judgeth it meete to grant this motion, and doe further desire & impower the wor'pfll Wm. Stoughton & Joseph Dudley, Esqs, to take particcular care & inspection into the matter of the land in the Nipmug Country, what titles are pretended to by Indeans or others, and the validity of them, and make returne of what they find therein to this Court as soone as may be." [1]

_____

[1] Mass. Col. Rec., V. 315.

This commission reported October 16th, 1681, that in June they had had a general meeting at Cambridge of all the claimants, but finding them at variance as to their several claims, they dismissed them until they could agree among themselves. They further reported,

"Since which time, in September last, perceiving a better vnderstanding amongst them, wee warned seuerall of the principall claymers to attend vs into the country, & travajle the same in company with us as farr & as much as one weeke would allow us, & find that the southerne part, clajmed by Black James and company is capable of good setlement, if not too scant of meadow, though vncerteine what will fall w'thin bounds if our lyne be to be quæstioned." [1]

They reported also upon lands in other quarters, but the action of the Court appears to have been taken only upon the Nipmuck lands. Stoughton and Dudley were empowered to treat with the owners thereof, and "to agree w'th them vpon the easiest termes that may be obtejned." [2]

On the 18th of February, 1681–2, another report was made by the agents to the Court, stating that

---

[1] Mass. Col. Rec., V. 328.–The boundary line between the Massachusetts and Connecticut colonies was at this time unsettled.

[2] Ibid. 329.

3

with the Hassanamesit and Natick Indians they had
agreed for all their land

"lying fower miles northward of the present Springfeild road,
& southward to that, haue agreed betweene Blacke James &
them, of which wee aduised in our late returne, wee haue purchased at thirty pounds money & a coate."

"The southern halfe of sajd countrey wee haue purchased
of Blacke James & company, for twenty pounds." [1]

The doings of Stoughton and Dudley were approved by the Court, and one thousand acres of land
were voted to each for their "great care & pajnes." [2]
These grants were surveyed by John Gore, at Manchaug, in one plat, and confirmed to them June 4th,
1685. [3]

In the act of General Court confirming this grant,
it is described as

"conteyning 1800 acres, with allowance of addition of two
hundred more next adjoyning, to compleat the same to 2000
acres, * * * in the Nipmug Country, at a place called
Marichouge [Manchaug] the lyne being marked w'th rainging
markes in the corners with S. D.," [the initials of grantees.]

According to the earliest plan in the Oxford Records,
"Manchaug Farm" measured 674 rods on its east and west
lines and 434 rods on its north and south lines. This
included both Stoughton's and Dudley's shares. A later plan,
made after the incorporation of the town of Dudley, in 1731,
gives "Manchaug Farm" as 1100 acres, the property of the

---

[1] Mass. Col. Rec., V. 342.   [2] Ibid. 343.   [3] Ibid. 488.

"heirs of Mr. Dudley" and "belonging to Oxford." A still later plan made in 1756 shows 1020 acres as in Oxford, and belonging to Thomas Dudley — and adjoining it on the east, in Sutton, is shown the balance of the plat as "now Richard Waters', and others'."

The deeds of purchase dated Feb. 10th, 1681-2, were presented to the Court May 27th, 1682, and received its confirmation. [1] The descriptions of the land conveyed are somewhat indefinite, but a careful study of the deeds leads to the conclusion that with Waban and company, Natick men, the bargain was for all the lands they claimed west of the Blackstone river, between the southern line of Massachusetts and an imaginary line commencing with the Blackstone river at a point four miles northerly of the Springfield road, and running south-westerly till it joined said Massachusetts southern line, and thus enclosing a triangle. [2]

[1] Mass. Col. Rec., V. 361.

[2] The description in the first deed is as follows :—"all that part of the Nipmug Country * * * lying, and being beyond the great ryuer called Kuttatuck, or Nipmug [Blackstone] Ryver, and betweene a rainge of marked trees, beginning at sajd riuer and runing south east till it fall vpon the south lyne of the sajd Massachusets colony on the south, and a certaine imaginary lyne fowre miles on the north side of the road, as it now ljeth, to Springfeild on the north, the sajd great riuer * * * on the eastward, and the sajd patent lyne on the westward." In the

With " Black James," the bargain was for the southern part of the same territory, designing also to include
lands which extended into what is now Connecticut.
These deeds were delivered at Natick, May 19th,
1682, and on the 27th the commissioners reported
that they had effected a purchase

"from the principall men of Naticke * * * of a parcell
of remote & wast land belonging to said Indians, lying at the
vtmost westerly bounds of Naticke, and, as wee are informed,—
is for quantity about — acres, more or lesse, being mean land." '

The consideration in the first deed was thirty
pounds, and the first signature was that of Waban,
who was chief at Natick. Twenty-two names were

second deed it is as follows : — "all that part of the sajd
Nipmug country *   * lying, & being on the south part
of the sajd colony of the Mattachusets, beyond the great riuer
* * * bounded with the Mattachusets patent line * * *
on the south, and certeine marked trees, beginning at sajd riuer
and runing south east, till it strike vpon the bounds *the* of sajd
patent line ; on the north, the sajd great riuer ; on the east, and
coming to a point on the west. " Mass. Col. Rec., V. 362—365.

The commissioners say in their report Feb. 1681-2, " The
whole tract in both deeds conteyned is in a forme of a
trjangle & reduced to a square, conteyneth a tract about fifty
miles long & twenty miles wide." Ibid. 342.

' Ibid. 361.

attached, probably representing the chief men of
the tribe living east of the Blackstone river. [1]

In the second deed the amount acknowledged was
twenty pounds. The first signature was that of
Black James of Chaubunagungamaug,[2] and the
twenty-nine other signers were doubtless inhabitants
of the tract conveyed. The black coat was given
to Black James as a mark of honor.[3]

[1] Waban was the first Indian chief who professed Christianity, and he entertained Mr. Eliot in his wigwam at his first
going among the Nipmucks. [Gookin.] He maintained a character for integrity and reliability which was recognized by the
state authorities, and was appointed a justice of the peace, or
"ruler of fifty," and was somewhat noted as a magistrate. The
following is a copy of one of his warrants :—

"You, you big constable, quick you catch um, Jeremiah
Offscow, strong you hold um, safe you bring um afore me.
—Waban, Justice of the Peace."

A young justice asked him what he should do when Indians
got drunk and quarreled. He replied, "tie um all up, and whip
um plaintiff, whip um 'fendant, and whip um witness." Allen,
Biog. Dictionary.

[2] This name signifies the "fishing place of the boundary,"
and was given to the large pond in the vicinity, which was
the boundary between the lands of the Narragansetts and
the Nipmucks.

[3] Gookin says, (1674,) of Chaubunagungamaug, "in this place
dwells Black James, who about a year ago was constituted

In the latter deed was a reservation to the amount of five miles square, for the exclusive use of this branch of the tribe, which might be chosen in two localities. The first was on the Quinebaug river at Maanexit, three or four miles southerly of Chaubunagungamaug, and the other, four or five miles southeasterly of Maanexit, in the present town of Thompson.[1] Most of the first named reservation was sold subsequently to Dudley or his heirs, and a part, at least, incorporated in the town which now bears his name.[2]

Associated with Stoughton and Dudley in public matters, and especially in efforts of a philanthropic nature, was another man of marked ability, and of great influence, not only here but in England— Robert Thompson, merchant, of London. This noble man became warmly interested in the success

------

constable of all the praying towns. He is a person that hath approved himself diligent and courageous, faithful and zealous to suppress sin."—A sale of land in the Quinebaug valley, Conn., was made by one " Hyems " or James, to the English, in 1653, and a coat was a part of the price paid.— Miss Larned, I. 5.

[1] Mass. Col. Rec., V. 488.

[2] " Five thousand acres at Quinnatisset and a large tract at Mayanexet, being a moiety or full half of the whole reservation, were immediately conveyed for the sum of ten pounds, to Stoughton and Dudley."—Miss Larned, I. 14.

of the New England colonies as early as 1650. and in 1670 was chosen president of the "Society for the Propagation of the Gospel in New England." [1] He had largely the confidence of the colonial authorities, and ably served the public interests both here and in England, and as a token of esteem a grant of land was made to him. as follows :

"This Court. being informed by our agents. now in England. of the good will & freindship of Major Robert Thompson of London. & his readiness upon all occasions to be assistants to them in the service of this colony. wherein they are. according doe. by way of gratuity. give unto the said Major Thompson & his heires. fiue hundred acres of land in the Nipmug countrey. to be laid out to him with all reasonable convenience." Dated May 16th. 1653. [2]

After his death the legislature of Connecticut granted two thousand acres to his grandson in London, as a tribute to his memory. [3]

Stoughton was also a man of wealth and high

---

[1] Hutchinson. I. 324.
[2] Mass. Col. Rec., V. 409.
[3] An old plan in the Oxford records shows. among other lots of land in the territory lying southerly of the town and northeasterly of Chaubunagungamaug pond. one designated as "Thompson's fiue hundred acres." Connecticut's grant was located in North Killingly. which place was afterwards chartered as a town. and named "Thompson." in honor of the grantee.

standing, and was in 1694 and 1700, acting governor
of the province. He was a liberal patron of Harvard
College, and his memory is perpetuated there in
the hall which bears his name.

Dudley was a leading spirit of his time. However
unfortunate he may have been in the direction
he gave to his influence, his eminent talents and
efficiency in public affairs cannot be questioned.
For many years his name appears in the records as
that of a man prominent in the management of Colonial matters, and especially in affairs pertaining to
the new settlements, where disputes were continually
arising on both civil and religious matters, his
services were often called into requisition by the
authorities. He held numerous high positions
under the government, and was governor of the
Province from 1702 to 1715. Stoughton and Dudley
were warm friends, and their names often appear
together in the Colonial records.

Associated with these gentlemen were Dr. Daniel
Cox, and John Blackwell, of London, [1] and Thomas

---

[1] John Blackwell was a member of parliament under Crom-
well, and a treasurer in his army. He was intimate with
Dudley while in this country, was made a justice of the peace
by him, and was often his adviser in public affairs.—Miss
Larned, I. 183.

Freak, of Hannington, Wiltshire, who were all men of influence, and were in sympathy with them in the plan of a settlement in Oxford, and intended to become themselves settlers in Massachusetts.

It is safe to affirm that hardly another colony, of the many which were then being projected, had such prospects of success, or so able and efficient guardians to watch over and aid it in its early struggles for existence and growth. It would seem that under the fostering care of such patrons, any enterprise which they might undertake would be sure to prosper. But in this case progress was very slow, and influences beyond the control of any set of men hindered the initiation of the scheme. Mr. Blackwell came over from England, and after remaining here several years, abandoned the idea of a permanent settlement in America, and returned. Dr. Cox and Mr. Freak gave up their intention of coming to this country, probably because of political changes which had taken place in Massachusetts, and also in England.

For two years after the date of the grant, no progress towards a settlement seems to have been made. The scarcity of men who met the demands of the grantees as settlers, and of such as had sufficient courage, zeal and ability to cope with the real difficulties in the way of establishing a colony in this frontier region, was doubtless a great obstacle in the way of progress. The demand for men in the older settlements was great, and especially in those which had been destroyed by the war, the proprietors were anxious to re-establish and re-build as fast as possible. The grant for Woodstock had been made November 7th, 1683, and so great were the obstacles, that in the spring of 1686, only thirteen men could be mustered who were ready to go.[1] Confidence in the peaceful professions of the natives had nearly vanished. The horrors of the recent war were still fresh in mind, and those who lived in the safer places near the coast were slow to go out and face the hardships of a pioneer life in a wilderness where roving bands of hostile Indians were scouting, and the resident tribes had proved themselves untrustworthy.

[1] Woodstock Rec.

CHAPTER III.

The grant for Oxford is as follows : —

"This court hauing information that some gentlemen in England are desirous to remoove themselues into this colony, & (if it may be) to setle themselues vnder the Massachusets ; for the incouragement of such persons, & that they may haue some from among themselues, according to their motion, to assist & direct them in such a designe, this Court doth grant to Major Robert Thompson, Willjam Stoughton and Joseph Dudley, Esq., and such others as they shall associate to them, a tract of land, in any free place, conteyning eight miles square, for a touneship, they setling in the sajd place w'thin fower yeares, thirty familjes, & an able orthodox minister, and doe allow to the sajd touneship freedom from country rates for fower yeares from the time aboue ljmitted." Dated May 16th, 1683.[1]

The survey of this grant was made by John Gore of Roxbury, and accepted by the General Court May 16th, 1683, and the place was named Oxford, after the city of that name in England.[2] The plan, a copy

[1] Mass. Col. Rec., V. 408.

[2] This fact does not appear clearly from the record, but receives

of which is now in the town clerk's office, comprehended forty-one thousand two hundred and fifty acres, or a little less than sixty-five square miles, and was two thousand one hundred and fourteen rods, or six and two-thirds miles on the easterly side ; three thousand three hundred and forty rods, or about ten and a half miles on the southerly ; one thousand nine hundred and sixty-eight rods, or about six miles on the westerly ; and three thousand two hundred and sixteen rods, or about ten miles on the northerly. The description in the deed of division—hereafter described—begins at the southwest corner of Worcester, which was near the present village of Auburn, and from thence the line ran nearly south, to the northwest corner of Mr. Dudley's grant of one thousand acres before alluded to,[1] and thence south fifteen degrees east, by the west line of said farm to

confirmation from the memorandum of Judge Sewall, of Boston, who in his diary wrote, "I gave New Roxbury the name of Woodstock, because of its nearness to Oxford, for the sake of Queen Elizabeth and the notable meetings that have been held at that place bearing the name in England." [Holmes' Annals. II. 449.] These places are about eight miles distant from each other, and are places of note in English history. At the University in Oxford many of the leading men of the early colonial times received their education.

[1] See map.

a point about one and a quarter miles southwesterly
of the village of West Sutton, and a mile and a half
west of Manchaug pond, known as "Manchaug Corner"—thence west fifteen degrees south, to a point
a little north of Peter pond in the easterly part of
Dudley, and thence continuing westerly, crossing the
Quinebaug river to a point in the vicinity of San-
dersdale, in the easterly part of Southbridge, thence
northerly to a point about two miles westerly of
Charlton city, on the Sturbridge line, thence easterly,
bearing northerly, to the southwest corner of Worcester.

These lines enclosed, besides the present town of
Oxford, nearly the whole of Charlton, about one
fourth of Auburn, one fifth of Dudley, and three or
four square miles of the northeastern portion of
Southbridge.

Through this tract there ran. due north and south,
a "way," twenty rods in width, called "the common
way." The design of this unusual provision can
only be conjectured, but as it is called on an old
plan the "proprietors' common way," it probably was
a reserve for the purpose of access to the several
allotments of the lands west of the village. We
find no subsequent allusion to it in the records, and
later, it is believed, it became a part of the village

territory, and its western line, the boundary. This
dividing line cut off from the main grant eleven
thousand two hundred and fifty acres of the eastern
portion, a tract six and two-thirds miles long, and
two and one-half miles wide, which was given to the
settlers for a "Village," or "General Plantation."

The remaining thirty thousand acres was divided
into five equal parts, the division lines running
easterly and westerly. These parts were allotted as
follows : the northernmost to Robert Thompson, the
second to Daniel Cox, the third to William Stoughton, the fourth to John Blackwell, and the southern-
most to Joseph Dudley. Mr. Cox's portion is sub-
divided on the plan between Blackwell, Freak and
Cox. All the bounds mentioned in this deed were of
a transient nature — marked trees, a heap of stones,
or a stake, constituting them all — except one, which
is permanent, and this was at the northeast corner of
the natural pond at the present Hodges' village.
This bound marked the "Village line," as it was
called. Mr. Blackwell's north line joined the Village
line at this point, so that the pond was in the northeastern angle of his portion, and is called on the
plan referred to, "Blackwell's pond." On another
plan of early date his share is designated as "now
Papillon's," and on another, later, as "Wolcut's and

"Williams'." [1] We have no record of the latter gentleman, but Josiah Wolcott, Esq., was prominent in the early history of the town, and was a grandson of Peter Papillon.

Thus it appears that Dudley, who became possessed of a considerable amount of landed property in this region, Stoughton, and Thompson — who had other lands in the vicinity — were the only three of the six original proprietors who had a permanent interest in the settlement of the place. The last two gentlemen seem — from the entire absence of their names in the records — to have given to Dudley the whole control of their interests, and down to the time of the permanent settlement by the English, he appears as the sole manager.

The deed of division referred to, is a document of much historical interest and value. It was found among old papers in London in 1872, and is now

[1] Blackwell, it appears, early disposed of his interest in the Oxford scheme and transferred his patronage to a new grant, which he obtained for himself and his English friends, January 28, 1685, located in the valley of the Quinebaug, near the present town of Pomfret, Conn.—Mass. Col. Rec., V. 467.

Stoughton's share is designated on this later plan as "now Brown's." But as his heirs signed the proprietors' proclamation in 1712, in reference to re-settlement, he must have retained his interest at the time of his death.

in the possession of the New York Historical
Society.[1]   It is dated July 3d, 1688.   A point of
peculiar interest in it, is in the description of Mr.
Dudley's portion, where it gives his northeastern
bound as a "white oak stake, square, driven in the
meadow, by the river which runs by and from the
French houses." This bound was about one-third
of a mile down this stream from where the road to
Webster now crosses it, and of course due south
from the northeast corner of the above named pond.
This is the only record we have touching the
existence of the houses of the French settlers at
that time, and it confirms what tradition says of

[1] This deed is on parchment, and is in good condition. It
is executed in a plain hand, with the prominent words and
phrases in Old English. Its size is two feet three inches, from
top to bottom, and two feet five inches in width, and it is closely
written to the margin. At the bottom is a fold inward of an
inch and a half, on which are placed at equal intervals five loops
of parchment, originally bearing seals in wax, now nearly gone.
The left hand seal bears the name Joseph Dudley, and the
second William Stoughton, the third and fourth are blank, and
the fifth has John Blackwell's signature.

It is witnessed on the back by Samuel Witty, Edward Thomas,
Daniel Bondet, I. B. Du Tuffeau, and William Blackwell. Du
Tuffeau's signature is excellent in style, and would do credit
to a modern business man. This deed is printed in full in
Amidown's Historical Collections, I. 128.

their location. Another fact of interest which we learn from this document, is the Indian name of the beautiful pond referred to, which was "Auguteback." [1]

---

[1] We cannot claim that this name is as charming as the lake which it represents, but as it was the name by which it was known by the aborigines, it is desirable that it should be retained.

Mr. Whitney gives it as "Augootsback," but there is evidence that the name in the deed is the one used by the early settlers.

While on the subject of names we would note that there is an obvious impropriety in calling the river running west of the village, the "French river." The tradition alluded to by Dr. Holmes, that part of the settlers located near that stream, is evidently erroneous, as it was outside the village line, and therefore not included in the grant, and if this were not the case it is altogether improbable that the small and comparatively defenceless body of men who came here, would scatter themselves over so large a territory as they must have done, had they settled there. The proper name of this stream is that given to it by the natives — "Maanexit."

The large, round topped hill, lying south-east of the village, called Mayo Hill, should be known by the name given to it in one of the first records made in the history of Oxford — "Bondet Hill."

4

CHAPTER IV.

At this point it is an interesting inquiry to raise, what were the natural characteristics of this locality which made it in Dudley's estimation, "capable of good settlement?"

It is well known that no part of southern central Massachusetts can boast of special fertility of soil. Its best lands are those of the hills which were originally covered with heavy growths of wood. The Oxford grant had in its western part, embracing most of the present town of Charlton, a large share of hilly country.[1] But its eastern portion, which was set apart for a village, was more level and capable of settlement, because of its meadows and plains. These plains extend about two and a half miles north and south,

---

[1] Mashamoquet or Mashamuckit Hill, near Charlton centre, is the most prominent point of land in the southern part of Worcester county, and is the highest in the range of hills running north and south, constituting the "height of land" between Boston and Springfield.

and embrace some five or six hundred acres, which have a warm soil of sandy loam, peculiarly adapted to the production of the chief crop of those early times, Indian corn. The country was not an unbroken forest, but here and there, especially on the plains, were open areas on which the Indians raised corn and other vegetables, and the Nipmuck region—especially its southern part—was early famous as a corn growing country.[1] Gookin said of Manchaug, "it is situated in a fertile country for good land," and further, he states that he had seen corn-fields in this region, yielding forty bushels to the acre. In the estimation of the settlers its value was decided by its ability to produce readily the means of subsistence; therefore the mellow and tractable soil of the plains was preferred to the more rugged land of the hills.

The natural meadows skirting the streams which ran on either side the plains, were considered the most valuable of all the lands, on account of the crops of hay they yielded.[2]

---

[1] Boston News Letter, Miss Larned, I. 2.

[2] Sudbury, Concord, Lancaster, and Brookfield were among the earliest inland settlements, and were chosen for their productive meadows.—The artificial pond in the eastern part of Oxford, called " Robinson's pond," covers what was one of the finest meadows in the vicinity, which has been known from the

Water power, an indispensible requisite, was here in a convenient location, and easily available.

Wild game, important as a means of living in those days, was plentiful in these forests, and fish were abundant in the ponds and rivers. We have it on good authority that the hills south-easterly of the village abounded in deer, and it is a matter of record that deer reeves were chosen annually in town meetings, in the early history of the town.[1]

Another favorable consideration was that this location was comparatively easy of access. The road

---

earliest history of the town, as "Mendon meadow," from the fact that Mendon people came there yearly to cut hay, before the settlement of Oxford.—See Addenda, B.

As late as the year 1828, it was the custom every spring, at a fixed time, to open the waste gates at the mill near the south end of the plain, and draw the water from the meadows above, that the crops of hay might grow and be harvested.

[1] Mr. Stephen Davis, recently deceased, at the age of eighty-seven years, said, on the authority of his father, that at the time of the settlement of his ancestors in the extreme south-east part of Oxford, a young man with a dog and gun could go into the woods near by, and bring home a fawn as certainly and almost as quickly as a farmer could go to his sheep-fold and prepare a lamb for use.

There were also here wild animals whose existence was not altogether desirable. Bears and wolves were not uncommon. "The Wabquassets paid to Uncas, Chief of the Mohegans,

from Boston to Springfield crossed the grant in its
northern section, and the old roadway to Connecticut
ran through its southern part.[1]

'yearly tribute of white deer-skins, bear-skins and black wolf-
skins.'"—Miss Larned, I. 3.

One condition of a certain treaty between Plymouth colony
and Philip was that he should deliver to the authorities annually
five wolves' heads.—Palfrey.

Mrs. Lee, in her "History of the Huguenots in France and
America," quoting from the manuscript of Mr. John Mayo, says,
"I heard Joseph Rockwood who served in the fort, tell of having
got lost in the woods when out for the cows. He heard at a
distance the cries of wild beasts, and ascended a tree for safety.
He was surrounded during the night by half famished, howling
wolves."

Tradition gives us the circumstances of the killing of two
large black bears in the vicinity of "Bug Swamp," in the
easterly part of the town, some twenty years after the settlement by the English.

[1] Gookin, in 1674, speaking of Hassanamesit, [Grafton,] says;
"It is near unto the old roadway to Connecticut." A glance at
the map shows that the most direct route from Grafton to
Woodstock is through Oxford, and we have further evidence
in this direction, in the fact that on a plan, dated 1711, of land
of Maj. Fitch, in the northern part of Windham County, the
"Connecticut path" is laid down as entering Thompson near
the middle of its northern boundary line, and near to where the
"Frenchtown river," as it is there called, enters it. The large
extent of Chaubunagungamaug pond renders this impossible,

The former way, called the "Bay path," had been
traveled for nearly fifty years, and was the thoroughfare between the east and the west, as they then
existed."[1]   Dr. Holland says of it :—

"It was a path marked by trees a portion of the distance,
and by slight clearings of brush and thicket for the remainder.
No stream was bridged, no hill graded, and no marsh drained.
The path led through woods which bore the marks of centuries,

---

unless the path came down on its westerly side, and this would
indicate that its course was through Oxford.

The fact that this "way" was called in the records the "great
trail," leads to the belief that it was originally the Indian path.
The probable reason for its bearing so far to the northward of
a straight line, was that the difficulties of crossing the "Medfield
river," might be avoided.   There is a record of a petition, very
early, for a bridge across this river.   The following is the action
of the Court :—

"Whereas, the way to Kenecticut now used, being very haz-
ardous to travellers, by reason of one deep river that is passed
fower or five times over, which may be avoided as is conceived,
by a better and nearer way, it is refferd to Major Pynchon to
order the said way to be laid out and well marked."—March
30, 1683, Mass. Col. Rec., V. 391.

[1] Distinct remains of the old "Bay road," for a third of a
mile or more, may be seen now in the "great valley" directly
west of Charlton Centre.   This fact is stated on the authority
of the late Gen. Salem Towne.

over barren hills that had been licked by the Indians' hounds
of fire, and along the banks of streams that the seine had never
dragged. * * * It is wonderful what a powerful interest
was attached to the Bay path. That rough thread of soil,
chopped by the blades of a hundred streams, was the one way
left open, through which the sweet tide of sympathy might flow.
Every rod had been prayed over by friends on the journey
and friends at home. If every traveler had raised his Ebenezer
as the morning dawned upon his trusting sleep, the monuments
would have risen and stood like mile stones." [1]

Miss Larned says of the "Connecticut path," "This rude
track became the main thoroughfare between the two colonies,
[Massachusetts and Connecticut.] Hundreds of families toiled
over it to new homes in the wilderness. The fathers of Hart-
ford and New Haven, ministers and governors, captains and
commissioners, government officials and land speculators,
crossed and re-crossed it."

The facts in the history of the beginning of the
sister colonies, New Oxford and New Roxbury, are
worthy of notice. Dudley had explored the sites of
both, and we have his opinion as to their promise for
settlement. The grant for Oxford had been made in

---

[1] This description applies to the "Bay path" as it existed
very early in the history of the colonies. At the time of the
settlement of Oxford it might have attained the dignity of a
wagon road. But Huntington, in his Centennial address at
Hadley, says that in 1675 the produce of the towns on the
Connecticut, was still sent down the river on its way to Boston.

May, 1683, and in November of the same year,
through the petition of thirty-six of Eliot's parish-
oners, townsmen of Dudley, the selectmen of Roxbury
received a grant in the same neighborhood,[1] with a
proviso that Thompson and company should have the
first choice of a location.[2]   While Mr. Dudley's pecuniary interests were mainly in New Oxford, his interest,
also, in the sister colony, was shown in the fact that
in town meeting at Roxbury he was chosen chairman
of a committee "to draft propositions that may be
most equal and prudent for the settlement of New
Roxbury."[3]   He was also instrumental in obtaining
for the New Roxbury settlers a deed of their lands
from the proprietor, Capt. James Fitch.[4]   Evidently
his valuable knowledge and experience served both
colonies, and no doubt his advice as to the management of the affairs of each was such as to insure
mutual sympathy and helpfulness.

More than two years elapsed after the New Roxbury grant was made, before settlers occupied either
place, and it is probable that the fact of the settle-

---

[1] Mass. Col. Rec., V. 422.

[2] Oxford's meadows, and the certainty of its being within
the bounds of Massachusetts colony, probably decided Stoughton
and Dudley in its favor.

[3] Roxbury Rec.   [4] Miss Larned, I. 19.

ment of the two towns in the same year was not accidental, and further it would seem not improbable that the receipt of the news of the agreement between Thompson and Bernon, in London, in the spring of 1686, concerning the settlement of Oxford, was the signal for the onward movement of the pioneers of Woodstock. We know that later, communication was free and constant between the two places.[1] The Chandlers, father and son, were leaders at Woodstock, and the records show that in all the region around, they were active in public matters, especially in the surveying and dividing of lands, and John Chandler, Jr., was in the list of the thirty English settlers of Oxford in 1713.[2]

---

[1] These places are about ten miles apart. Woodstock Hill is plainly visible from the site of the Oxford fort, and it is believed that intelligence passed between them by means of signals, at these points.

[2] John Chandler, Jr., although one of the thirty grantees of the Oxford Village, probably never settled here. He took a share in the enterprise, it seems, as a speculation; he, and also his father, being extensive operators in land in all the towns adjacent to Woodstock. He disposed of his interest here in the latter part of 1714. He was chosen colonel of the militia, and in public affairs he became the most influential man in this region. It was through his instrumentality chiefly, that Worcester County was established in 1731. At its organization he

In the course of events it became necessary for the
people of Oxford to garrison themselves for protection against the Indians. Woodstock then furnished soldiers to assist as guards.[1]

---

took the post of honor, and was appointed Chief Justice of the
Court of Common Pleas, and also Judge of Probate. He con-
tinued to live in Woodstock until his death in 1743. Dea.
John Chandler, Sen., died in 1703.

Oxford had the offer of being made the county seat of the
new county, but declined the honor, on the ground, it is said,
that the influences of a shire town would endanger the good
morals of the young people.

[1] Humphrey to Holmes. "Memoir of French Protestants
who settled in Oxford, Mass., 1686," by A. Holmes, D. D.
—Mass. His. Soc. Col., Vol. II. 3d Series, p. 80.

This most interesting memoir, the first and only account
of the Oxford Huguenots heretofore published, is now out of
print, and very rare outside of the libraries.

CHAPTER V.

In the spring of 1685, no progress appears to
have been made towards occupying the Oxford
grant, and on the petition of the grantees, the
stipulated time for making the settlement was
extended three years.[1] Before the expiration of
this time the problem was solved, and the requisite
number of settlers from a people of a strange country and language, and a most remarkable history,
were here as colonists. We cannot enter at length
into their record before their emigration. It is a
long, dark and bloody history, a story of conflict
and intolerance, of suffering and heroic endurance.
An imperfect outline must suffice.

The Reformation in France had its beginning
among the young men of the University at Paris,
under the lead of Jacques Lefevre, about the year

---

[1] Mass. Col. Rec., V. 469.

1493.[1] The work had made considerable progress before John Calvin came upon the stage, and when, in 1530, he appeared as a champion of the truth, large numbers hailed him as a leader, and enlisted under his banner. Under him the progress of the cause was rapid, and many of the noblest men of the nation, including some very near the throne, became its adherents.[2] In 1550 the balance was so nearly poised that it was doubtful whether the Huguenots would not gain control of the government. Three bloody civil wars ensued in quick succession, in which the Protestants suffered great losses. In 1570 the noble Henry of Navarre, afterward King Henry IV., was their principal hope as a political protector. In 1572 he married the sister of the king, and from all parts of France the leading Protestants were invited to Paris to attend the

---

[1] "The father of the French Reformation, or the one more than any other entitled to this distinction, is Jacques Lefevre, born in Picardy about 1455."—Fisher's Hist. Ref. 277.

[2] "Coligni greeted him as a leader of the Reformation. * * * His system of doctrine and polity * * * gave comfort to the Huguenots, shaped the theology of the Palatinate * * * controls Scotland to the present hour, founded the Puritanism of England, and has been the basis of New England character."—Appleton's Cycl.

nuptial ceremonies. Then occurred the massacre
of St. Bartholomew, that dark blot in the world's
history, in which two thousand persons in Paris,
and twenty thousand in the kingdom, were killed
in eight days. Terrible as was this blow, its effect
was only to arouse and bring together more closely
these people, and under their favorite, Henry, the
conflict was renewed, and carried on with varied
results till 1589, when he came to the throne.
Upon assuming its responsibilities, as a measure of
policy and conciliation he joined the Catholic church,
and nine years after, he issued the famous Edict of
Nantes, which gave religious liberty throughout the
land. In 1610 Henry died, leaving the Protestants
politically defenceless. Persecution began again
soon after his death, and the Edict was practically
annulled. Cardinals Richelieu and Mazarin, particularly the latter, —until his death in 1651— were
influential in partially restraining the persecutions.
But on the accession of Louis XIV., in the same
year, the clouds quickly gathered, and all the ener-
gies of the government were directed toward the
extermination of the heretics. By means of bribery
and dragooning, in which the Protestants suffered
untold atrocities, many were forced to abjure their
religion, and in form, the Reformed church was

almost destroyed before the revocation of the Edict in 1685. But when that blow fell, a proof was given of the power of the Faith to hold its adherents. When the choice came between conformity to the State religion and expatriation, hundreds of thousands accepted the latter, and bade a last farewell to their native land.[1]

These refugees are said by historians to have been among the very best people of France. As men of character and moral worth they were eminent. In comparison with the Puritans they were as firm and well-established in their religious opinions, as devout, less bigoted, yet more cultivated and refined. They were intelligent in religious matters, profound Bible students, and also excelled in music, having a metrical translation of the Psalms, and the hymns of Beza, and of Marot,—who was called the French Watts, — set to the sweet harmonies of Goudimel, an early French composer.

As artisans in silks, glass, rich jewelry and pottery, they have never been excelled, and to this day

---

[1] The number of French refugees who left within a few years after the Revocation, has been very differently estimated at from two hundred and fifty thousand to eight hundred thousand, but most authors agree in stating it at about five hundred thousand.

the best workers in these materials in London are
their descendants.

"Spittlefields and the parts adjoining," says Stowe, "became
a great harbor for poor Protestant strangers, Walloons and
French, who, as in former days, so of late, have been found
to become exiles from their own country for their religion, and
for avoiding the cruel persecution. Here they found quiet and
security, and settled themselves in their several trades and
occupations, weavers, especially; whereby God's blessing is
surely not only brought upon the parish, by receiving poor
strangers, but also a great advantage hath accrued to the whole
nation, by the rich manufacture of wearing silks, and stuffs, and
camlets, which art they brought along with them. And this
benefit also to the neighborhood, that these strangers may
serve for pattern of thrifty honesty, industry and sobriety."

Near Leicester Square is a house of worship called "the
Orange Street Chapel," built in 1684 by subscription, for the
French Protestants.

"Within its walls they prayed for the Prince by whom they
had been forbidden to follow their trades and professions, forbidden Christian burial, and exiled, and whom yet they re-
spected as the Almighty's scourge." [1]

Smiles, in his History of the Huguenots, says: "They were
acknowledged to be the best agriculturists, wine-growers,
merchants and manufacturers in France. No heavier crops
were grown in France than on the Huguenot farms in Bearn,
and the south-western provinces. The slopes of the Aigoul and

---

[1] Hare. Walks in London, II. 128.

the Epernon were covered with their flocks and herds. The valley of the Vaunage was celebrated for its richness of vegetation, and was called by its inhabitants the "Little Canaan." * * * The diligence, skill and labor with which they subdued the stubborn soil and made it yield its increase of flowers and fruits, and corn and wine, bore witness in all quarters to the toil and energy of the men of the Religion."

Of these refugees, fifty thousand went to London, others to Holland, to Brazil and other parts of the western continent. They settled in Florida, New York, Massachusetts, Rhode Island and Virginia, but more than in any other State, in South Carolina. In all these places they assisted in laying firmly the foundations of our noble institutions, and to use the language of a recent writer, " They have contributed in proportion to their numbers, a vast share to the culture and prosperity of the United States." He adds, "they were noted for severe morality, great charity, and politeness and elegance of manners." [1]

We learn from the records that America was early held in high esteem by these people, and that for a number of years before the crisis came, their eyes were directed to this country as a place of refuge, and inquiries were sent as to the prospects for emigrants, especially for those who tilled the soil. [2]

---

[1] Appleton's Cycl.   [2] Holmes, 28.

The chief agent in their removal hither was
Gabriel Bernon, a merchant of Rochelle,[1] who having fled to London after the Revocation, was there
introduced to Mr. Robert Thompson, by an eminent
French gentleman then in that city. The result was
an agreement on the part of Mr. Bernon to make the
settlement on the Oxford grant, of the thirty French
Protestant families.[2] He did not manage the affairs
of the colony in person, but employed as his agent,
Isaac Bertrand Du Tuffeau, to whom, on his arrival
in this country, as a matter of encouragement, was
given as the representative and co-partner of Mr.
Bernon, a tract of seven hundred and fifty acres
of land in New Oxford.   Subsequently, at the
solicitation of Du Tuffeau, Mr. Bernon came to
Boston, when a further grant was made to him in
his own right, of seventeen hundred and fifty acres,
making twenty-five hundred acres in all, the whole
lying within the village plat, and embracing more
than one-fifth of its whole extent. [3]

---

[1] La Rochelle was for many years the stronghold of the
Protestants in France. It is situated on the sea coast, and is
the port of a fertile region which produces largely, grain, wine,
cattle and horses. Most of the company which came to Oxford
are believed to have been natives of this place or its vicinity.

[2] Holmes, 69.   [3] Ibid.

5

CHAPTER VI.

THE history of this enterprise, from the time when the emigrants left France to the breaking up and extinction of the settlement, is difficult to trace, for want of documentary evidence. Diligent search among the records of England and this country, has failed to bring to light much which is satisfactory as to its detail. The few facts we have, are drawn from isolated papers, letters, petitions and documents of various purport, gathered from many different sources, which give us only glimpses, from time to time, of the progress of events in the settlement. The "books, papers, and acts of the village," which M. Bondet, their minister, is charged with having taken away when he left, although they have been diligently sought for, have never been recovered. Tradition gives us but few facts. Enough, however, of the enterprise is known to throw around the subject a romantic interest, which is rare in New England history.

Dr. Snow, in his history of Boston, says that during the summer of 1686 a number of vessels having on board French refugees, arrived at that port. Among these are believed to have been many of the company who afterward came to New Oxford.[1] As the requisite number of emigrants did not occupy the grant at the beginning,[2] we infer that the company was not organized until their arrival in Boston, although as Bernon certifies that he "paid the passage for over forty persons to America,"[3] it is probable that a part, at least, left Europe with direct reference to the settlement here. The colony was founded in 1686.[4] Arrived on

---

[1] It is extremely probable that some of the first men in New England aided these proscribed Rochellese in their emigration. —Holmes, 29.

[2] See letter Fr. Prot. Refugee in Boston, 1687, page 72.

[3] Letter to Gov. Shute. Holmes, 69.

[4] It has been claimed by some that the settlement was made in the spring of 1687, but we see no reason for doubting the statement of Whitney and of Holmes that it was in 1686. Bondet, in his letter to Cornbury, 1702, says that he had then been in America about fifteen years. This is indefinite. When he particularizes and says he was nine years in Oxford, two years waiting in Boston, and five years in New Rochelle, we have sixteen years, which gives 1686 as the time of settlement. The fact that collections in behalf of the French refugees in Boston were

the location of the proposed settlement, they fixed upon the eminence a mile and a half south-east of the present centre of the village, as their head-quarters. At this point, for many years afterward, the highway from Boston entered the town. At a short distance to the south-east from this spot, upon higher ground, overlooking all this region, was the site of the large fort. The large round-top hill lying just below the fort, is called in the records "Bondet hill." From this we conclude it was owned by him while living here. On its eastern slope, just at the entrance of the Boston road, stood what is called in the records the "Great House." This is believed to have been Bondet's residence.

Of their church building no relic or mark remains, but its location is fixed with certainty by tradition.

_____

taken up in Salem and other places in the fall of 1686, proves nothing on this point, as there were those who remained per-manently in Boston, (see letter Fr. Ref., page 72,) and others went to colonize other parts of our country.—Snow.

These people were in straitened circumstances and could not consult convenience, and considering that the Woodstock settle-ment had been begun, it seems more probable that the pioneers, at least, went at once to their destination, than that they remained in Boston, living on charity through the autumn and winter of 1686–7.

Within the memory of persons now living, there were to be seen large stones, said to have been part of the foundation of the building, upon the first rise of ground on the left, after crossing the stream, on the road from the village to the fort, about sixty rods south-easterly of the Humphrey homestead.[1] Near the church, easterly from it, was their burying ground, and a small fort or palisade was built in the immediate vicinity, for protection in case of an attack in time of religious service. [2]

Among the first things to be provided, were mills to furnish lumber, and for grinding grain. These were located upon the stream east of the "Plain," the principal stream within the village bounds; one near the south end of the present Main street, called in the records the "old mill place," and the other a short distance below what is now Rich's mill, known as the upper site. From the little light we get from

[1] This homestead was the first residence of Ebenezer Humphrey, who came from Woodstock to Oxford while the French were here, to keep garrison, (see Holmes, 80.) and is the place referred to in a vote in town meeting, Jan. 25, 1714.—See Addenda E.—It has remained in the family since the settlement in 1713, and is now owned and occupied by Ebenezer Humphrey, of the fourth generation from the first of the name. It is the only homestead in the town, which remains in the possession of the family of the original owner.

[2] Addenda F.

the records, we conclude that the first mill built was a saw-mill, at the lower site or "old mill place." In the Village Proprietors' records the lower site was called in 1714, "the old mill," and also "the old mill place," which indicates that the first attempt to locate a mill was at this place. This was nearly in the centre of the population. Later, as it would seem, the grist-mill was built, at the upper site.

The plantations were chosen chiefly upon the plains; and upon their eastern borders, near the meadows and running stream, they built their houses. These were placed with no regard to order or regularity, but each on a spot best suited to the taste of the owner.

That there was real beauty in the plan on which the settlement was built, is readily seen. Above the whole, overlooking the valley for miles, was the main fort. Just below was Bondet hill, which, in its turn looked down on the church and lower fort, which stood at its foot. Still lower were the meadows, with the picturesque river winding through them, and beyond, on the higher banks, scattered up and down were the dwellings, and stretching behind these were the level plantations, and the receding forest hills made up the background.

Disosway in his "Huguenots in America," says, "The different parts of the country to which they came were greatly benefited by the introduction of their superior modes of cultivation of the soil, and of different valuable fruits which they brought from France. * * * When Charles II. in 1680, sent the first band of French Protestants to South Carolina, his principal object was to introduce into that colony the excellent modes of cultivation which they had followed in their own country."

Lawson — an early traveler in the south — says "Their lands presented the aspects of the most cultivated portion of France and England."

From these, and other evidences of their skill in cultivation, it is easy to believe that during their residence here, these people wrought a great change in the aspect of the place, and that by their well directed labor, wide and fertile fields, and fruitful gardens were made to flourish, where before existed only the unprofitable growths of the original forests.

CHAPTER VII.

To trace its progress as far as possible, we now take up in order of time, the documents we have referring to the colony after its establishment. The earliest date is that of a letter of a French Protestant refugee in Boston, published by the French Protestant Historical Society,[1] dated Nov. 1687.

[*Translation.*]

"The Nicmok Country belongs to the President, himself, (referring to Bernon, probably,) and the land costs nothing. I do not know as yet the precise quantity that is given to each family; some have told me it is from fifty to a hundred acres, according to the size of a family. * * * It lies with those who wish to take up lands whether to take them in the one or the other of the plantations — on the sea-board or in the interior. The Nicmok plantation is inland, at a distance of twenty leagues from Boston, and equally distant from the sea; so that when the settlers wish to send anything to Boston, or

---

[1] Bulletin, XVI. 73.

to obtain anything from thence, they are obliged to transport it in wagons. In the neighborhood of this settlement there are small rivers and ponds abounding in fish, and woods full of game. M. Bondet is their minister. The inhabitants as yet number only fifty-two persons."

In this remarkable letter we find mention of some of the prominent facts in the early history of this enterprise, — that land was furnished free to the settlers, and that their support was to come from this land by their own skill and hard toil, and that no better inducement could be offered them to choose a home here, than "woods full of game, and ponds and rivers abounding in fish," and "fifty to a hundred acres" to a family, chiefly of rude and unsubdued forest land, twenty leagues away from civilization.

There was, however, an alternative. As early as 1685, a band of refugees had gathered at Boston, over which Laurent Vandenbosch officiated as pastor,[1] and it lay with the emigrants to choose to remain there or to go to settle the Nipmuck lands. We know but little of the sea-board colony, as its

---

[1] Rev. Charles W. Baird, D. D., sketch of Pierre Daillé, in Magazine of American History, Vol. I. p. 94.

distinctive history was early merged in that of the growing town of Boston, but it is probable that the quantity of land they might occupy there was comparatively very small.[1]   But the brave hearts and the strong arms which were needed to meet the stern realities of the case were not wanting. In the second year, in spite of all discouragements, fifty-two persons had made a home in the wilds of the Nipmuck country, and the pastor, Bondet, was with them to counsel and cheer them in their new and trying experiences.

The allusion to carrying in wagons, is the earliest intimation we have of any means of conveyance other than by horseback. If a wagon road existed, it could have been little more than a broad bay path.[2]

---

[1] Tradition informs us that the Huguenot settlers in Boston made the most of their grounds, and to a considerable extent gratified their taste in the cultivation of rare and beautiful fruits and flowers. The will of Andrew Johonnot, dated 1759, gave to Mrs. Johonnot a part of his estate, comprising rich gardens and finely cultivated grounds, filled with the choicest fruits, shrubs and flowers, natives of France.

"A friend, now no more, Daniel Sargent, Esq., told me he perfectly recollected fine gardens pointed out to him when a boy, as having belonged to the Huguenots."—Mrs. Lee, II. 68.

[2] On a plan dated April 1, 1713, in the Massachusetts

Our second date is that of the deed of Dudley
and the other proprietors, to Bernon, which is May
24th, 1688.[2]   This document, with the deed of
division which was executed forty days afterward,
— July 3d, 1688, — we take as evidence that the
full quota of thirty families was settled on the plantation in the spring of this year.   The stipulated time in
which this was to be done, had expired in the January previous.   We have no intimation that a request
for a further extension of time was made, and the
simple fact of the deed to Bernon being drawn,
would indicate that he had fulfilled his part of the
contract.   We also find in the deed itself evidence
in the same direction, as in the consideration, no
allusion is made to the completion of the contract
to settle the thirty families, but it simply requires
that he should build a mill for the use of the inhabitants.   We find, also, strong confirmation of
this fact in the doings of the proprietors, in dividing
their lands, a thing they would not be likely to do
while the main condition on which they held their
grant was uncomplied with.

Archives, of a grant of land to Jethro Coffin, located in North-
bridge, there is laid down, easterly and westerly, a line designated
as "the French road."— Plans and Grants, I. 240.

  2 For this Deed, see Addenda K.

Next, in order of time, is the "contract of Mr. Church, for the mill for New Oxford." [1]

From this it appears that in the third summer of the colony's existence the much needed mill was erected, although from the date of the latter receipt it seems probable that it was not completed until the winter of 1689–90.

From the agreement on Bernon's part to furnish boards, we have ample evidence that the saw-mill had been built, and furthermore, his agreement to make, erect and finish the dam, is proof that the projected grist-mill was to occupy a new location, which the records indicate was the upper site.

The next paper is dated July 6th, 1691. This document, although bearing upon matters pertaining to the Indians, rather than the colony, is interesting as introducing Rev. Daniel Bondet, and showing something of his spirit and work. He being at that time their religious teacher, was exceedingly tried by the results of the rum traffic.[2]   He says :

    "The rume is always sold to them without order and meas-

---

[1] For this "Agreement" see Addenda L.

[2] M. Bondet was at this time not only pastor of the French Congregation, but also missionary to the Nipmuck Indians, under the direction of the "Society for the propagation of the Gospel in New England."

ure. * * * The 26th of last month there was about twenti
Indians so furious by drunkness that they fought like bears,
and fell upon one remes * * * who is appointed for
preaching the gospel amongst them: he had been so much
disfigured by his woads that there is no hope of his recovery.
If it was your pleasure to signifie to the instruments of that
evil the jalosie of your authoriti and of the pablique tranquility,
you would do great good maintaining the honor of God in a
Christian habitation, comforting some honest souls wick being
incompatible with such abominations feel every day the burden
of affixon of their honorable peregrination aggravated. Hear
us pray, and so God be with you and prosper all your just
undertakins and applications.

'tis the sincere wish of your most respectuous servant.

                                    D. BONDET.

Minister of the gospell in a French congregation at New
Oxford." [1]

The Selectmen of Woodstock, following Bondet's
precedent, the next February, sent to the Court a
similar petition, appealing for relief.—

"Whereas there are many Indians belonging to To-ke-ka-mo-
woo-tchong and others who have been resident in this town
for a long time who are often times very drunken: to the great
dishonor of God, the grief of good men, the prejudice of themselves and other Indians who are often beaten and bruised and
almost brought to death's door, a sad example whereof hath
been the last week in our town and its evidence enough by the

_____

[1] Holmes, 61.—The first part of this paper, including the address, is lost.

Indian testimony who the persons are of whom they obtain
their drink; here is none here in authority who may punish
such offences, which might be a good mean to prevent
such disorders as we account ourselves in duty bound, do
inform your Honor and pray that some order be given, as your
wisdom shall judge meet, that for the future such woful
practices may be prevented.

WOODSTOCK, Feb. 22, 1691-2.

JOHN CHANDLER,

WILLIAM BARTHOLOMEW,

BENJAMIN SABIN,

EDWARD MORRIS,

Selectmen.[1]

In 1693, Daniel Allen was chosen representative
from New Oxford, to the General Court at Boston.
According to Mr. Whitney, a special act of this body
was passed, authorizing this action. We do not find
the record of this act, but Mr. Allen's name appears
in the list for 1693 as from this place. [2] The list
for this year numbers sixty-eight. Fifty-nine of these
were from that portion of the Province east of the
present Worcester county. In this county, Lancaster, Mendon and Oxford were represented. From
west of these places there were only six representatives, all from the Connecticut valley.

---

[1] Mass. Arch. XXXVII. 308.   [2] Gen. Court Rec., 278.

Mr. Allen appears February 6th, 1690, as a witness of the deed from Dudley and others, to Bernon,
but we have no other mention of him in connection
with the colony.   He is recorded as being "of Oxford," but as the name is not French, we conclude
that he was an Englishman interested in the place, and
well acquainted with its wants, and better fitted than
any Frenchman, with slight acquaintance with the
English language, to represent it in the legislature.
The fact that there are in the records other names
not French, connected with the affairs of the colony,
—as Johnson, Ingall and Evans—leads to the belief
that to some extent the English associated with the
Huguenots in the settlement.

Down to this time, affairs had, apparently, gone on
favorably, and the colony had made steady progress
in wealth and general prosperity.   But a reverse was
at hand, as will be seen from our next paper, which
sets forth vividly the state of affairs at the time it
was written.

The new town, having by the Provincial government been granted the privilege of representation,
was justly required to submit to taxation.   Accordingly, in 1694, a moderate assessment was made and
sent, with an order for its collection, to the "Constable of the French Plantation."

The following was sent in reply to this order:

[*Andrew Spooner v Sir William Phips, esq.*]

"To His Excellency Sir William Phips, Knt. Capt General and Governour in Chief of their Majesties Province of the Massachusetts Bay in New England, and to the Honourable Council ".

"The humble petition of Andrew Spooner, Constable of the French Plantation.

"Humbly sheweth unto Your Excellency and to Your Honors that your petitioner received an order from Mr James Taylor Treasurer for collecting eight pounds six shillings ... whereas the Indians have appeared several times this Summer, we were forced to garrison ourselves for three months together and several families fled so that all our Summer harvest of hay and corn ... grow ... by the bears and ... which had brought us so low that we have not enough to supply our own necessities ... other families abandoning ... likewise so that we have none left but Mr ... our minister and the ... of our plantation ... that we are incapable of paying said Poll unless we dispose of what little we have and quit our plantations. Wherefore humbly entreat this Honorable Council to consider our miseries and incapacity of paying this poll and as in duty bound we shall ever pray "

Mass Archives, C 300 — Payment was not entered. We ... at ... "abating, remitting and forgiving" taxes ... this place ... amount of forty-three pounds and six shillings — Province Laws 1694 p 5.

This paper has no date upon its face, but is
endorsed. " Read Oct. 16. 1694."

The period from the founding of the colony in
1686 to the spring of 1690, may appropriately be
called the planting time. From 1690 to the spring of
1694 there seems to have been gradual growth, and
prosperity — this was the season of its flourishing.
In this petition we have the premonition of the
coming end. In the declaration " the Indians have
appeared." is revealed the cause of the decay and
final extinction of the settlement. Its decline began
with the disasters set forth in this appeal. It would
seem that the Huguenots had an instinctive dread of
the natives. The stories of their terrible barbarity
and cruelty in the late war were doubtless current
among them, and it needed only to be known that
Indians were lurking in the vicinity, to send fear and
trembling through the community.'

' The sensitiveness of the people to the approach of the
savages was doubtless increased by an incident, the main facts
of which form the basis of one of the stories which Mrs. L. H.
Sigourney has given, with much elaboration, in her " Legend
of Oxford." Two children of M. Alard, whose dwelling stood
near the old mill site, were in the woods gathering nuts or ber-
ries, when a company of Indians came upon them, captured
them, and took them away. It was not until after two or three
days' search that they were found and returned to their home.
— Mrs. H. Daniels.

Upon an alarm being given, they forsake their homes and plantations and hasten to their stronghold for safety, and there remain three months; while the wild deer of the forest, and the cattle — which then were allowed to range at large — make havoc of their promising fields of grain, their fruits and thriving gardens.

The loss of crops in 1694 must have made the winter following a hard one, and the abandonment of their plantations by the best men of the settlement, of course had a very disheartening effect on those who remained. Another discouraging fact, was, that not long after the date of this petition, for causes which now cannot be known, M. Bondet, their pastor, also left them and returned to Boston. [1]

For a year and ten months after the date of this petition the history of the colony is a blank, and we

[1] In proof of this, we cite, first — the direct statement of the "Inhabitants of Oxford" in their petition to General Court, through Laborie, to this effect, [p. 88.] Next, Bondet's statement to Lord Cornbury, in his letter, 1702, that he had then been away from Oxford seven years, [p. 120.] As corroborative, we have his letter to Mather, dated New York, Jan. 10th, 1698, [p. 118,] which proves—if he spent two years in Boston after leaving Oxford — that he was there January, 1696, which was eight months before the breaking up of the colony.

have no means of knowing the condition of things
in this critical period of its existence. The fact,
however, that Bondet did not return, gives ground
for the belief that there was little or no improvement.

The next record we have concerning New Oxford
is that of the Johnson massacre, Aug. 25th, 1696.
This tragedy decided the fate of the colony. The
house of Johnson stood apart from the rest of the
village, southward, on what has been known since
the time of the massacre as Johnson's plain, about
a mile and a quarter south of the present Town
Hall, near the Webster road. Tradition says that
a small band of Indians of some hostile Western
tribe, toward the close of the day, stole upon the
dwelling, and, entering it stealthily, seized three
young children of the family, and killed them, by
crushing their heads against the stones of the fire-
place. With the help of her brother, the mother,
in her terror—her first thought going toward her
absent husband—fled southward toward Woodstock,
whither he had gone on business. hoping, probably,
to meet him on his return. It is said that in parts
of the way there were two paths, and that in going
and coming the husband and wife passed each
other, she going on to Woodstock, and he coming

to his home to be met and killed at his own door
by the murderers of his children. [1]

---

[1] "It has been conjectured that John Johnson was a Frenchman, whose name had been Anglicised. The impression is
mistaken. He was a native of Alveton, or Alton, county of
Stafford, England." — Dr. Baird.

He married Susan Sigourney, the daughter of the constable.
After her return to Boston she married, April 18th, 1700, her
cousin, Daniel Johonnot, born in France. — Sigourney Genealogy, 8.

Johnson's house was kept as a tavern, being near the Woodstock "great trail." — Mayo's Manuscript.

Dea. Ebenezer Humphrey is quoted as having said that the
friendly Indians informed his father that the perpetrators of this
deed were the Maquas, or Albany Indians. The opinion pre-
vails that this is an error, and that they were Canadian Indians.
The fact that they were traced to the vicinity of Worcester,
immediately after the massacre, strengthens this theory. —
See letter of Daniel Fitch to Governor Stoughton, August
31st, 1696.

The names of these children,—Andrew, Peter, and Mary,—
are preserved to us by tradition. — Mrs. H. Daniels.

Two others, Goodman Servin and John Evans, are some-
times mentioned as victims of this massacre.— Olney's Address
at Dedication of Memorial Hall.

A rough stone monument was erected by an assembly of the
people of Oxford, on the site of the Johnson house, Aug. 25th,
1875, the one hundred and seventy-ninth anniversary of the
massacre. Dr. O. W. Holmes, in answer to an invitation to

Reduced and waning as the settlement was at this date, it is not surprising that such an attack should fill the people with dismay, and bring them to an immediate determination to leave, and seek a place of safety. Hastily gathering together the few valuables they might take with them, in great fear lest the attack should be renewed, the whole company returned to Boston.

The story of their leaving is full of touching interest, and has been often repeated among the dwellers in Oxford in olden times. Tradition says that early in the morning of the day of their departure — each family having bade adieu to its plantation and home — they assembled at the church, where they had a season of worship. They afterward repaired to the burying ground to take leave of the graves of departed friends, and

be present, wrote : "The occasion you propose to celebrate is a very interesting one, in an exceptional kind of way, and deserves an orator quite as much as many more widely-known events of real history. * * * I should think the day might be made interesting and delightful. * * * I must content myself with sending my most cordial good wishes to my friends of the lovely town which records so touching, beautiful, and romantic a story in its annals."

then, in a procession, moved onward over the
rough forest road toward Boston. [1]

The scene presented on that August morning, of
the leave-taking at this sacred spot, was a remarkable one. Standing there in imagination, it requires
but little effort to see, as we look westward across the
meadows, the lonely houses with their closed doors
and blank windows. Near at hand stands the rude
chapel, where, but just now, the farewell prayers and
songs have been offered up. In the middle fore-
ground are the graves of the dead, and here and
there, friends bending tearfully over them. In the
front is seen a large, newly-made mound, and by it
stands the central figure of the whole scene. She,
who but yesterday was the happy wife and mother
of those who now sleep their last sleep beneath it,
stands pale and trembling under her weight of grief,

---

[1] In 1819 Mr. Andrew Sigourney wrote to Prof. Brazer, of
Cambridge, that, according to Capt. Ebenezer Humphrey's
statement, on his farm, as his father told him, there had been a
fort, and also a French meeting-house, and a burying-ground,
with a number of graves : that he had seen the stones that were
laid on the top of them — as we lay turf — and that one of the
graves was much larger than any others. — Holmes, 80.

Captain Humphrey informed Mrs. Stearns DeWitt, that the
larger grave was that of Johnson and his children. He also
gave the number of graves, from recollection, as about twenty.

leaning upon the arm of the father, who, in paternal tenderness and sympathy bends over her, and tries with words of love to soothe the sorrows of the stricken child. By her side stands the faithful brother, and a little apart are grouped around the friends, whose tearful eyes tell of the common feeling of pity and sympathy which fills them all.

We shall have to look far in New England history to find an incident more full of dramatic interest and genuine pathos than this. [1]

[1] The attack upon New Oxford had its effect upon the Woodstock settlement also, and caused some to leave the place in alarm; while those who remained, sought the protection of General Court. Thirty-eight days, only, elapsed after the massacre, before an act of that body was passed, as follows:

October 2d, 1696. "Upon information given that several of the inhabitants of Woodstock have lately removed, and that others are about to remove from said town, whereby the duty of watching, warding, and scouting will lie too heavily upon those that do remain, and endanger the place to be exposed, being an out plantation — Ordered, that the said town of Woodstock be accounted a frontier, and comprehended within the act of the General Assembly, entitled the 'Act to prevent the deserting of frontiers,'" etc. — Gen. Court Rec., 1696, p. 481.

Under this act settlers were forbidden to leave, and frontier towns were garrisoned and fortified to some extent, and commissioners appointed to consult with military officers in such places, with reference to all matters pertaining to their defence.

CHAPTER VIII.

But this was not, in fact, the end of the French occupation. Tradition informs us that a part, at least, of those who left in 1696, returned and re-settled the place. That which rested long upon tradition only, has now documentary evidence to support it. The re-settlement was probably made as early as the Spring of 1699. The first paper we have touching this point, is the petition of the "Inhabitants of the town of New Oxford," by James Laborie, their minister, dated October 1st, 1699.

[*James Laborie " Tou His Excellencie and tou the Honorable Council."*]

MY LORD AND MOST HONORABLE COUNCIL :

" Mr. Bondet, formerly minister of this town, not only satisfied to leave us almost two years before the Indians did commit any act of hostility in this place, but carried away all the books which had been given for the use of the plantation, with the acts and papers of the village, we most humbly supplicate your Excellency and the most Honorable Council to oblige

Mr. Bondet to send back again said books, acts, and papers belonging to said plantation.

"The inhabitants, knowing that all disturbance that hath been before in this plantation, have happened only in that some people of this plantation did give the Indians drink without measure, and that at present there is some continuing to do the same, we most humbly supplicate your Excellency, and the Honorable Council to give Mr. James Laborie, our minister, full orders to hinder those disturbances which put us in great danger of our lives. The said inhabitants complain also against John Ingall, that not only he gives to said Indians drink without measure, but buy all the meat they bring, and goes and sell it in other villages, and so hinders the inhabitants of putting up any provisions against the Winter. We most humbly supplicate your Excellency and most Honorable Council to forbid said John Ingall to sell any rhoom, and to transport any meat out of the plantation that he hath bought of the Indians, before the said inhabitants be provided.[1]

[1] We have mention of John Ingall in the Council records, in February of the same year.

"His Excellency also acquainted the board that by express from New Oxford, he had received a letter from Lieut. Sabin of Woodstock," concerning the Indians who had gone eastward, as was believed, with the purpose to join others in plotting mischief. — Council Rec., 94.

"Advised and consented that his Excellency issue forth his warrant to Mr. Treasurer, to pay forty shillings unto John Ingall, sent with an express from Oxford bringing the news." February 7th, 1699.—Ibid., 95. We infer that Ingall was chief

"James Laborie in his particular most humbly supplicate your
Excellency and the most Honorable Council to give him a peculiar order for to oblige the Indians to observe the Sabbath day,
many of the said Indians to whom the said Laborie hath often
exhorted to piety—having declared to submit themselves to said
Laborie's exhortations if he should bring an order with him
from your Excellency, or from your honorable Lieutenant
Governor, Mr. Stauton, or the most Honorable Council.

"Expecting these favors we shall continue to pray God
for the preservation of your Excellency, and the most Honorable Council," etc.   JAMES LABORISH."

This petition is endorsed "Lre, written 1st Xbr 99 w'th a
proclama'con for the observance of the Lord's day inclosed."[1]

We have no record of the doings of the authorities
upon this petition, but, from the following letter,
conclude that they required of Laborie a certificate
from the inhabitants, substantiating the charges
against Bondet.

[*Monsieur Laborie to the Earl of Bellomont.*]

"At NEW OXFORD. this 17th June, 1700.
"MY LORD:

"When I had the honor to write to your Excellency,
I did not send you the certificate of our inhabitants with

trader in Oxford, and brought goods from Boston, selling to
colonists and Indians, and that with the latter, rum was a leading article of trade, in exchange for wild meats, furs, etc.

[1] Mass. Arch., II. 140.

reference to Monsieur Bondet, for the reason that they were not
all here. I have at length procured it, and send it to your
Excellency. As to our Indians, I feel myself constrained to
inform your Excellency that the four who came back, notwithstanding all the protestations which they made to me upon
arriving, had no other object in returning than to induce those
who had been faithful, to depart with them. They have gained
over the greater number, and to-day they leave for Penikook,
— twenty-five in all,— men, women, and children. [1]   I preached
to them yesterday in their own tongue. From all they say, I
infer that the priests are vigorously at work, and that they are
hatching some scheme which they will bring to light so soon as
they shall find a favorable occasion." [2]

[*Earl of Bellomont to the Lords of Trade, London.*]

[July 9, 1700.]

"Mons. Labourie is a French Minister placed at New Oxford
by Mr. Stoughton, the Lieut. Gov'r, and myself, at a yearly
stipend of £30, out of the Corporation money; there are eight
or ten French families there that have farms, and he preaches
to them." * * *

"The Indians about the town of Woodstock and New Oxford,
consisting of about 40 families have lately deserted their houses,

[1] Pennacook was a dwelling place of the tribe of that name,
at the present site of Concord, New Hampshire.

[2] The priests here referred to, were the Jesuits of Canada.
They were doubtless jealous of the influence of the French
Protestants upon the natives in this vicinity, and were doing all
in their power to draw them away to themselves.

and corn, and are gone to live with the Penicook indians, which has much allarmed the English thereabouts, and some of the English have forsaken their houses and farms and removed to towns for better security. That the Jesuits have seduced these 40 families is plain.   *   *   *   Mr. Sabin is so terrified at the indians of Woodstock and New Oxford quitting their houses and corn, that he has thought fit to forsake his dwelling and is gone to live in a town.   All the thinking .people here believe the Eastern Indians will break out against the English in a little time." [1]

A list of "such as receive salary for preaching to the Indians," has " Mons. James Laborie, at Oxford,   £30. 00. 00." [2]

Another record touching the re-settlement, is the petition of the French Protestants in Boston, asking aid for their church, dated June 29th, 1700, and signed by Peter Chardon and René Grignon, "elders of the French Congregation." A part of this petition is as follows :—

"Considering also that your humble petitioners have borne great charges in paying taxes for the poor of the country, and in maintaining their own poor of this town, and those of New Oxford, who by the occasion of the war withdrew themselves, and since that they have assisted many who returned to Oxford, in order to their re-settlement." [3]

The next paper touching this point, is the letter of

[1] Doc. His. State N. Y., IV. 684.
[2] Ibid., 755.—For incidents of Indian history, see Add. N.
[3] Mass. Arch., 11, 150.

Governor Dudley to Bernon, in reply to his petition for aid in the protection of his property against the Indians, dated July 7th, 1702, which is as follows :—

"Herewith you have a commission for Captain of New Oxford. I desire you forthwith to repair thither and show your said commission, and take care that the people be armed, and take them in your own house with a palisade, for the security of the inhabitants; and if they are at such a distance in your village that there should be need of another place to draw them together in case of danger, consider of another proper house, and write me, and you shall have order therein.

"I am your humble servant,

"J. DUDLEY."

From the request for the return of the "books, papers and acts of the village," in the foregoing petition, we infer that the first colony was a body politic, transacting business in a public capacity, having officers, and enacting rules for the government of its affairs, and also that the pastor of the church was public clerk, and the custodian of the records. [1]

We learn also, that drunken Indians at this time, as well as eight years before, were the terror of the Huguenots, and this appeal for relief, under the

[1] A general law of the province authorized small towns to govern themselves until they became large enough to come under the provincial laws.

declaration that all their disturbances were due to the sale of rum, evidently came from an honest conviction that there was no quiet or safety for them until it could be abolished.

Further, we learn that the forest was an important source of supply of food to the people, through the Indian hunters and the local trader.

Lawson, before referred to, says of the Huguenots, as he saw them in Carolina, "they live like a tribe, like one family; and each one rejoices at the elevation of his brethren." [1] In the petition of the French elders, we have revealed the same admirable trait of character. They possessed as a class, a spirit of large-hearted benevolence and charity. The secret of their genuine nobleness lay in the fact that their religion was not mere sentiment, but a living principle which controlled their lives.

From this paper we gather further, that the second colony was made up of those who belonged to the first, also.

The last document, the letter of Gov. Dudley, is proof that there was serious trouble in 1702. The Indians were again menacing the place, and the writer evidently felt that there was need of some one here having military authority, that the people might

[1] Disosway, Huguenots in America.

be so directed that they might be able to defend themselves and their property. The requisite authority was given, in a manner indicating that serious fears were felt that another breaking up was near.

That this alarm was felt, also, in the Woodstock colony, is shown by the fact that Lieut. Sabin, of that place, reported to the Massachusetts Council, April 9th, 1702, that the Indians were plotting mischief, and that he had ordered a garrison to be put in repair, and a military watch kept. The Council approved his doings, and cautioned him that while he kept watch he should do nothing to provoke the Indians, or cause them to think harm was intended to them. [1]

Another date in the Council Records enables us to trace the second colony to the summer of 1703. Soldiers were here for its protection from the savages who still hovered around.

"An accompt of wages and subsistence of thirteen soldiers, whereof one a sergeant, posted at Oxford and Hassanamisco in the summer past, was laid before the board and there examined and stated the whole sum, with other incidental charges amounting to forty pounds, fifteen shillings, three and a half pence."

"Ordered paid Dec. 24th, 1703." [2]

[1] Council Rec., 500. [2] Ibid, 509.

There is evidence that Bernon had business transactions with people living in New Oxford, in 1704. [1]

The same year Laborie was called to New York
as pastor of the French Reformed Church in that
city.

Of the further history of the colony we have no
record. The combined efforts of the government
and the proprietors failed to sustain its waning
interests. The final abandonment certainly ensued
soon thereafter, for in 1713, in the deed of the proprietors to the thirty English settlers they declare,

"Forasmuch as the said French families have many years
since wholly left and deserted their settlements in the said
village, and the said lands as well by their deserting the same,
and refusing to return upon publick Proclamations made to
that end as by the voluntary surrender of the most of them,
are now reinvested in and restored to * * * the original
proprietors,"

They therefore gave, granted and confirmed them
to the English settlers. [2]

---

[1] Bernon Papers.—Dr. Baird.

[2] About ten families only of the Huguenot settlers of Oxford
can now be traced, — Sigourney, Maillet, Grignon, Baudouin
and Faneuil to Boston : Bondet, Martin and Du Tuffeau to
New Rochelle, and Dispeux to Rhode Island. — Dr. Baird.

CHAPTER IX.

Between 1704 and 1712, the date of the proclamation of the proprietors calling for new settlers, we
have two important letters.[1] From these we learn
that Dudley and Bernon were each alive to the
preservation of their interests in the deserted plantation. The latter being aware of the necessity of
holding possession, sent here, as agents or tenants,
one Cooper, and a "negro Tom," to occupy the
premises, and to carry on some of the simpler farming operations. These men managed badly in
Dudley's estimation, and were guilty of wanton
disregard of his rights, as appears in the following
letter :—

[*J. Dudley to G. Bernon.*]

BOSTON, 20th May, 1707.

"Sr: I am very unhappy in my affayres at Oxford, both
with your Cooper & the negro Tom. I must desire you to

[1] Bernon Papers.—Dr. Baird.

7

take other care of your affayres than to improve such ill men that disquiet the place, that I have more trouble with them than with seven other towns. If you do not remove them yourself, I shall be obliged to send for the Negro & turn him out of the place, & I understand Cooper is so criminal that the law will dispose of him. I pray you to use your own there not to Destroy or Disturb the Governour or your best friend, who is, Sr., your humble servt.,

" J. DUDLEY.

"Send an honest man and he shall be welcome. I pray you to show what I write to Mr. Grignon."

" To Mr. Gabriel Bernon, Newport, Road Iland."

From the transactions which followed, we infer that soon after the date of this letter, Bernon came to Oxford. The result of this visit was an engagement with new tenants, which might be less objectionable to Dudley. His agreement with them was written on the back of the foregoing letter, which fact fixes its date as subsequent to May, 1707.[1]

We hear nothing more of Oliver and Nathanael Coller as Bernon's tenants.[2]

They could not have remained as such more than one or two years, as will be seen by the letter which follows. Bernon now complains against Dudley's

---

[1] For this agreement, see Addenda O.

[2] Oliver Coller was one of the thirty English settlers.

agent, Hagburn, and charges him with serious inter-
ference with his interests.[1]

[*G. Bernon to Gov. Dudley.*]

PROVIDENCE, 1st March, 1710.

[*Translation.*]

" Mr. Dudley your son told me the last time I had the honour
to see him, that it was your Excellency's design to re-establish
New Oxford : as it also appears through the public news.

" I hope your Excellency will be so good as to take into consideration the fact that Mr. Hoogborn has done his utmost to
ruin my interest in the said Oxford.

" He has caused Couper to abandon the old mill, and Thomas
Allerton [to leave] my other house, threatening that he would
hinder them from haying, and [declaring] that I had no power
to settle them.   When I made complaint of this to him he told
me that he would drive me from the place, myself.   Thus it is

---

[1] Samuel Hagburn was one of the thirty English settlers, and
was the first named in the deed of Dudley, etc., to them.   In
1726 an entry was made of an extract from his will, on the records of the Congregational Church, by which, although not a
member of it, he bequeathed to it the sum of fifty pounds.   For
a period of one hundred and ten years his name was as familiar
as household words, in the church, in connection with this gift.
In 1836 it was voted to apply it toward the expense of building
a church chapel.   This building was afterward sold, and the proceeds applied towards the finishing of the lecture-room as it now
is, in the basement of the meeting-house, and no more is heard
of the " Hagburn Fund."

that I have been treated, after spending at the said Oxford more than fifteen hundred pistoles [and] the better part of my time during more than twenty years possession.[1]

"Should it please your Excellency to examine the case you will find that I have chiefly had at heart the furtherance of your Excellency's wishes. I have been found singularly attached to your person, more than to all else that I have had in the world.

"It is notorious that the said Mr. Hoogborn your brother, has caused the planks of my granary to be torn up: that he has conveyed them elsewhere, and that by his orders the oxen that I was reserving to be fattened, have been put to work."

From this document we learn that notwithstanding Dudley's censure of Cooper, he remained in the place, and had lately been in possession of the farm called the "Old Mill," and that he, as well as the Collers, had been induced to leave it by Hagburn, acting probably under instructions from Dudley, whose aim evidently was to prevent Bernon's holding by possession, a property so important to the prosperity of the town. This farm had, no doubt, been granted to him as builder and owner of the

[1] In several instances in his papers we find Bernon laying stress upon the fact of his *possession*, from which it is evident that he was relying upon it to establish his proprietorship in the lands which he occupied, which were not conveyed to him by deed.

mill, on conditions of which we have no knowledge.
But Hagburn, we find, was now in possession. The
positive manner of his treatment of Bernon's tenants,
his ordering affairs concerning the granary and oxen,
his declaration that Bernon had no power to settle
these men, and his threat that he would drive him
from the place, show clearly his intention.

Bernon seems to have been wanting either in the
courage or the tact requisite to contend success-
fully with this opposition. With what grace he
yielded, appears from his reply to Dudley, who, in
answering the above letter, had intimated that there
was a prospect of disposing of a part of the Oxford
property.

[*G. Bernon to Gov. Dudley.*]

"PROVIDENCE, 19 Apr. 1710.

"Your Excellency, always benevolently disposed, informs me
that you purpose to obtain for me a good price for one-half of
that which I own in the village of Oxford. I wish to defer
entirely to your counsel. Accordingly I will proceed to Boston
as soon as possible to pay my respects to your Excellency." ₁

These expectations were never realized.

In 1715, two years after the settlement by the
English, he gave the stones and irons of the grist-

₁ Bernon Papers. — Dr. Baird.

mill to Daniel Elliot, one of the settlers, on condition
that he should build a mill in a specified time.[1]

[*Gov. Dudley to G. Bernon.*]

"ROXBURY, Apr. 6th, 1715.

" SIR :

"We are now in a way to thrive at Oxford, and I particularly thank you for what you have done toward a grist-mill
in the village, by giving the mill stones to Daniel Elliot, condi-
tionally that the mill should be built to serve the town within a
prefixed time, which is now past and nothing done. I desire
you to write to him to go forward immediately, so as to finish
the mill presently to the satisfaction of the Inhabitants, or that
you will order the said mill and irons to be given to such other
person as will go forward in the work, that they may not be
starved the next winter.

" I pray you take effectual order in the matter.

" I am your humble servant,   J. DUDLEY.

" To Mr. Gabriel Bernon, Narragansett."

In his reply, Bernon says he has "ordered Daniel
Elliot to finish the crist-mill at Oxford or to let the
town have the two mill stown, to set the mill in a
convenient place," adding significantly—pathetically,
almost—"it will be a great blessing to strive [thrive]
after so much distorbance."[2]

---

[1] Addenda D.

[2] Holmes, 66. The mill having been built twenty-five years,

In October, 1720, the following letter was written :

[*G. Bernon to the Son of Gov. Dudley.*]
"SIR :

" I would entreat you to assist me in petitioning his Excellency and the General Assembly, inasmuch as the inhabitants of New Oxford oppose my rights to lands.

" The Court and Government can confirm my title, and then I can dispose of what I have there, and pay my debts and have wherewithal to help myself; and thereby ease my mind and body — which is now more than the Pope can do.

" The above said inhabitants oppress me, as I can make it

---

had at this time become unserviceable from disuse and decay. The clause referring to its being set in another place, indicates that its location was not convenient.   The " convenient place " was at the lower site, where it was afterwards built.   That there was a grist-mill at that place in the early history of the town, is proved by tradition.—Mrs. H. Daniels, on the authority of her father, born near the spot.

Mr. Larned Davis, who lived to old age near the upper mill site, and who died in 1869, said :   " I have an impression that the grist-mill was removed from the upper to the lower site."

January 15th, 1715, Ebenezer and James Elliot were voted into the right of their father, Daniel Elliot.   This was the " old mill right."— " said lot being where the saw-mill is."   [Town Rec.]   This was three months before Bernon gave the stones and irons to Elliot, and ordered him to go on and build a mill. The upper mill was on land claimed by Bernon.   There is not the least probability that the town would grant rights there.   We take this as evidence that the saw-mill was at the lower site.

appear by Maj. Buor, who would have bought my plantation.
The inhabitants told him not to do it: — that my title was
nothing worth, that they also pretended that they would dispute
my title with Mr. Dudley and Mr. Thompson. They also
abused me in a very outrageous manner in Maj. Buor's presence; as he states in his certificate, which I make bold to send
to you enclosed in this.

"Ephraim Town, John Elliot, and John Chamberlin, for
whom I have advanced considerably to uphold my said plantation, will not pay me what they owe me. Besides, the loss of
my servant, who was drowned, was fifty pounds loss to me. [1]
These men, and one Josiah Owen, my last tenant, hugger-mug-
ger together to cheat me of a hundred pounds in cattle and
movables that I had upon the place, so that I am not able to
advance any more.

" I see myself about ruined by this oppression and malice.
Sir — you are perfectly acquainted with the affairs at New
Oxford, and I do not understand things as well as I would.
Therefore I intreat of you, Sir, to help me. Your charity and
generosity are (so to speak) interested in it.

" I am so hard driven by my dunning creditors—the masons
and carpenters and others that I employed to build my house
in Providence, that I know not what to do: and, besides my
wife now lying in, six or seven children implore my compassion, which makes me implore that of Government, and yours,
Sir, that my title may be confirmed, after a possession of 36
years, so that I may sell it. Within 30 years I have laid out on
it £200, for which reason my family did slight me, as well as

---

[1] This is the first record we have of a slave in Oxford.
Was this the negro Tom?

my best friends. I have always been protected by Mr. Dudley, your honored father, who always thought as I did, that I might sell it, and not be in any wise molested. But I don't know whether it won't be a mistake. Indeed, one cannot always foresee the events of things, often hid from the wisest. But this I see,—the Evil one still reigns, and God suffers it, to try his children.

"My great desire is to keep myself in the fear of God, and to love my neighbor, and to seek lawful means to maintain my family. My great age of nearly eighty years does not dispense me of this duty. I address myself to you with all humility to assist me, that I may be assisted by the Governor. Such a testimony of your love and favor will rescue me, to terminate my days in America, or to return once again to Europe. Surely my staying or going depends upon the action of the Assembly. But be it as it will, Sir, as an honest, well-minded man ought, I pray for the Government, and all the faithful in Christ.

"GABRIEL BERNON.

" From my chambers at Mr. Harper's.

　" adjoining unto Judge Sewall's, Oct. 1720." [1]

From this letter it is evident that at its date he was still retaining possession of improved property here—probably the fort and surrounding lands,—upon which he had employed men, to " uphold" it. Town was one of the thirty English settlers, and there

---

[1] Bernon Papers. — Dr. Baird.

were five families named Chamberlin and two named
Elliot among them.

In November, 1720, he made his application to
Gov. Shute for reimbursement of money spent upon
the colony. This petition is printed in the "History
of the Narragansett Church," and also in substance
in Holmes' Memoir. In it he says he came to Boston
"allured" by his agent, Du Tuffeau, who wrote him
exciting letters ; that

"on his arrival he was granted an additional seventeen hundred
and fifty acres of land, making twenty-five hundred acres in
all, * * * * for more authentic security his * * *
Excellency and Honor was pleased to accompany [him] to
Oxford and to put [him] in possession of said land, * * *
[and he] spent above two thousand pounds to defend the same
from the Indians who at divers times have ruined the plantation, and have murdered men, women and children. [That he
had] built a corn miln. [from the French, *moulin*] a wash leather
miln and a saw miln, and laid out some other considerable
expenses to improve the town of New Oxford."

This petition was accompanied by certificates
signed by some of the prominent men of Boston,
and also by some of the former residents in Oxford,
attesting the correctness of its statements.

We have no record of the result of this application.

The peculiar conditions under which Bernon held
his property in Oxford made his claim liable to
dispute, and, perhaps, with an honest belief that he
had no legal rights, "unlicensed settlers began to
occupy and claim his forest lands," thus causing him
much annoyance.[1]   But as a town, Oxford never
questioned his right to the original grant.   Among
the first matters which came before their public
meetings, was that of the settlement of the lines
between his property and the Village.   In Sept.,
1714. it was voted that "the committy shall take
care to notify Mr. Gabriel Bernon to come and
join us in settling division lines between us and
him."[2]   Again in Oct., 1718. a similar vote was
taken.[3]

But there was a good reason why this matter was
not attended to by Bernon.   The complicated nature
of the case is shown in his deed from Dudley and
company.   Du Tuffeau, at the beginning of the settlement had "elected" seven hundred and fifty acres,
which were deeded to him and Bernon jointly.
Afterward, to Bernon, seventeen hundred and fifty
acres were granted, which were deeded to him in his
own right, and also to Bondet were deeded two

---

[1] Allen's Mem.   [2] Prop. Rec. 3.   [3] Ibid, 27.—Addenda J.

hundred acres.[1]   These grants were all embraced in one plat and conveyed as a whole.   We have no intimation of a mutual division, and without this, no power but a court could give to either of the grantees an indisputable right to a single acre which should be set off and located.

Another point which is shown in the deed, added to the complications, namely ; that a very valuable portion of the land taken up and occupied by Du Tuffeau and Bernon, jointly, was not included in the conveyance.   This was a long triangular tract of nearly five hundred acres, lying between Bernon's land, as deeded, and the land of the village proprietors.   Its westerly line ran over the high land between the site of the fort and Bondet hill, and continuing in a course north, thirteen degrees east, crossed the present Sutton road at the fork, about three-fourths of a mile easterly of Main street.   This line is called in the town records, " Bernon's line,"[2] and has been marked on the western boundary of the estate now known as the Ebenezer Rich farm, by permanent division fences to the present day.

.

---

[1] We have no proof that Bondet ever had possession of this grant or received any benefit from it.

[2] Addenda F and G.

On this tract were the fort and the grounds around
it, where Bernon had expended considerable money,
and the upper mill site.   It also enclosed some of the
best farming lands within the limits of the town.   Of
course Bernon was anxious to retain it, but he could
plead possession only, as ground of ownership.   In
conveying his property he followed the deed he had
received from Dudley and company, and did not
include the disputed tract. [1]

Du Tuffeau having died before the autumn of
1720, Bernon applied to the probate court of Suffolk
county for a letter of administration on his estate, as
chief creditor. [2]   This was granted Dec. 5th, [3] and
he was enabled in due course of law thereby to take
possession of the twenty-five hundred acres as sole
owner.   Negotiations with Thomas Mayo, Samuel
Davis and William Weld, all of Roxbury, soon
followed, and a sale of the tract was made to them

---

[1] There is among the Bernon papers a plan of his Oxford
property.   In it the boundary at the southern part of the west
line as deeded, is indicated by a dotted line.   Westward of this,
running obliquely, so as to enclose the disputed triangular tract
is a *full* line, purporting to run N. 13° E., but which is plainly
wrong in drawing.   Here we have additional evidence that he
claimed the land as originally taken up by Du Tuffeau.

[2] Bernon Papers.—Dr. Baird.   [3] Suffolk Prob. Rec.

early in the Spring of 1721, for twelve hundred pounds, current money of New England. [1]

On March 27th, 1721, at a meeting of the Village proprietors to hear what the "Gentlemen which signifie that they have bought Mr. Bernon's farm have to be communicated to the inhabitants and proprietors of Oxford village," and to "act as shall be thought best to come at their own rights:"—

---

[1] The quantity of land sold was twenty-five hundred acres, and the description in the deed is as follows : "Beginning at a walnut tree marked S. D., standing at the south west corner of Manchaug, and thence running west, fifteen degrees south, three hundred and fifty-two perches, from thence to be set off by a line to be drawn parallel to the utmost easterly line bounds of the said Oxford village and township, as far as will complete the full quantity of twenty-eight hundred and seventy-two acres."

Of this were reserved one hundred and seventy-two acres of meadow in one piece, which Dudley gave to the village. But the two hundred acres for Bondet's farm are not mentioned. A provision in it required the annual payment of forty shillings quit-rent to Dudley, etc. This deed was dated March 16th, 1720–1, and is recorded in Suf. Co. Rec. XXXV. 119.

It is said that Weld, coming to see the premises in the spring after the snow had gone, was dissatisfied, and soon after sold his share to Davis.

"Thomas Mayo never came to Oxford, but his son John did, and Samuel Davis came in 1728 or 9, probably the latter."— Letter of Hon. George L. Davis, of North Andover.

"Voted and chose Dea. John Town, Benoni
Twichel, and Isaac Larned" to act as a committee
to establish the line between the said farm and the
village, and instructed them to "improve" John
Chandler, Esq., as surveyor.

The report of this committee, dated Apr. 11th,
1721, was accepted at a meeting of the proprietors,
Sept. 21st, 1721.[1] In accordance with its terms, a
portion of land at the north end of the Bernon
tract was released to the Village, and the triangular
plat which had been in dispute was yielded to the
purchasers.[2]

John Mayo, son of Thomas, made a home on the
height near the fort, and died there, and his descendants continued to occupy the premises until within
about twenty-five years. Davis chose for his dwelling, a spot nearly half a mile northerly from the fort,
on the farm now known as the Nathaniel Davis
place, where he died, and his descendants have had
possession to the present time.[3]

The facts in connection with the delivery of the

---

[1] Prop. Rec.—Addenda I.

[2] See dotted line on the map.

[3] Persons now living in Oxford well recollect the leaden sash
and the small diamond panes of glass of the old windows of this
house, which many years ago gave place to more modern ones.

deed to Bernon are remarkable. It will be remembered that it was drawn May 24th, 1688, probably
upon the completion of the contract to settle the
thirty families. There was in it, however, a consideration which had not been rendered, namely, the
building of a grist mill, for which reason it was not
at once delivered. A little less than two years
passed, the mill was built, and Bernon had Church's
receipt for the same. Two days after the date of
this receipt, we find two of the grantors acknowledg-
ing the deed before a magistrate—but still it was
not delivered. Years passed ; the first colony flourished a while and became extinct — the second
colony began and continued five years and was
abandoned — for nine years afterward the plantation
lay waste. Then the thirty English families came in
and laid the foundations of a permanent settlement.
Bernon gave up his right in the mills, and gave the
valuable stones and irons for the benefit of the new
colony. At last, after his hopes and expectations
had been again and again disappointed, and he had
grown old, and become unable for lack of means
to assist the settlement further, on Feb. 5th, 1716,
nearly twenty-eight years after the deed was written,
it was acknowledged by Dudley, and passed over
to him.

Six days afterward, Feb. 11th, 1716, he conveyed the property for a thousand pounds to James Bowdoin,[1] who held it until March 16th, 1720-1, when he re-conveyed it to Bernon,[2] who the same day executed the deed to Mayo, Davis and Weld.

Whether Dudley did not consider himself authorized to complete the conveyance until a permanent settlement was made, or Bernon declined to accept a deed which did not embrace valuable lands which he held in possession,— or whether it was withheld as a means of influencing Bernon, or some other reason existed, does not now appear. But in reviewing the transactions in the partial light of the present, we can hardly withhold our sympathy from Bernon, nor avoid the conclusion that in business matters he had, in Gov. Dudley, more than his equal.

---

[1] Suf. Rec., XXXI., 79.

[2] This conveyance was made by returning the deed he had received, with an endorsement upon it in legal form, signed, sealed, and witnessed by John Mayo, Samuel Tyler, Jr., and acknowledged before John Chandler, Justice of Peace. — Ibid.

8

CHAPTER X.

Our knowledge of the men who were actively
engaged in this enterprise is exceedingly limited,
with the exception of Bernon. A considerable collection of his papers remains, to this day, in the
possession of his descendants, extracts from which
have been published in several historical works.[1]

He was of an old and honorable family in
Rochelle, where he was born in 1644. "He was
possessed of a large property there, and was heredi-
tary registrar of the city."[2]   He was imprisoned two
years for his independence in religious matters, and
after the revocation of the Edict of Nantes left his

---

[1] Rev. Dr. Holmes had access to them repeatedly, and published, in his memoir of the Huguenots, many interesting facts
gathered from them.   The History of Narragansett Church
also contains extracts from them, and Zachariah Allen, L.L.D.,
Bernon's great grandson, prepared from them a manuscript
memoir of him.

[2] Potter's Hist. Narragansett, 314.

country and the greatest part of his estate, [1] and fled to London, from whence he came to America. He had a large family of daughters, whose descendants are among the first families in Providence. His only son died young. [2] " His memory is respectfully cherished in the hearts of his descendants." [3]

Mrs. Lee calls him an excellent man, and says his memorials are very interesting. The obituary notice referred to, continues :

" He was courteous, honest and kind * * * and has left a good name among his acquaintances. He evidenced the power of Christianity by leaving his country and his great estate, that he might worship God according to his conscience."

However estimable he may have been as a friend and a citizen, as a business man he was not successful. He was not lacking in enterprise, for he

---

[1] Obit. notice, Boston, July 19th, 1736, in Hist. Nar. Chh., 60.
[2] Hist. Nar. Chh., 59. [3] Ibid. — He had a brother, Samuel Bernon, who was a wealthy merchant, doing business between Rochelle and Quebec, where he owned large stores. [La Hontan.] This man was a bigoted Roman Catholic, and wrote to Gabriel in his old age, on religious and family matters, a remarkable letter, full of censure and reproach. — Mrs. Lee's Huguenots in France and America, II., 122.

projected a variety of business schemes; but it would seem that in the novel and changed circumstances in which he found himself in this new country, his judgment of affairs was faulty, and most of his experiments proved failures. His investments in New Oxford were the occasion of heavy pecuniary loss to him, and were a source of much trouble and anxiety in his old age.

According to his own representations to Gov. Shute, he had engaged in ship-building, in nail making, and the manufacture of stuffs and hats. One project of his was the extensive manufacture of naval stores from the pines which abounded in this locality. [1] About the year 1693, he petitioned the king of England for a royal patent, or order to supply his majesty's ships with resin, pitch, tar and turpentine, representing that he had "spent seaven years time and labour, and considerable sums of money, and has attained to such knowledge and perfection as that said commodities have beene bought for your Majesty's stores." He also states that he had made

---

[1] We find from the records that in 1723 complaint was made to the General Court by the people of Oxford, that trespassers were guilty "of bleeding trees for tar," on the adjacent province lands. A law was passed prohibiting it.

two voyages to London with express reference to
this business. [1]

He never lived in Oxford, but resided in Boston
during the existence of the first colony, and removed
in 1698 from thence to Newport, R. I., and soon
afterward to Narragansett, where he remained eight
or nine years. From that place he removed to
Providence, where he died in 1736, at the age of
ninety-two years. He espoused the cause of Episco-
pacy soon after leaving Boston, and was very zealous
in promoting its interests, being a leader in the
organization of the first church of this denomination
in each of the three above named places.

While the colony at its commencement was
dependent for material subsistence upon Bernon, the
most influential man in it appears to have been
Pastor Daniel Bondet. From his official position,
education, and the ease with which he acquired
the use of the English language, he is believed to
have filled a considerable place in the secular as well
as the religious affairs of the village. There is the
best of testimony to the fact that he discharged his
varied duties with faithfulness, and that in his life he
was pure and upright. He received from the society
under whose direction he labored, a salary of twenty-

[1] Bernon Papers.—Holmes, 68.

five pounds per annum, [1] and his people paid him an annual stipend of forty pounds. [2]

He was descended from a noble family, his mother being a daughter of Philippe de Nautonnier, Sieur de Castelfranc. Of him, Quick wrote : "This gentleman preaches in three languages unto three several nations — English, French, and Indians. " He espoused a most virtuous lady of a ducal family in France. [3]

Dr. Baird in writing of him, says :—

"My impression of Bondet is that he was a worthy and well-meaning man, but by no means a man of much strength of character. The people of New Oxford seem to have had some grievance against him in connection with his removal from them."

The following unique letter, has, we believe, never before been printed :

[*D. Bondet to Increase Mather.*]

"NEW YORK, the 10 Jan., 1697-8.
" DEAR SIR : —

" It is an old and innocent custom to use words of congratulation at the revolution of the year : we are as travellers in the

---

[1] Heathcote's letter.   [2] Mrs. Lee, II. 62.
[3] Agnew's Prot. Exiles from France, II. 164.

world, and the use * * *   to the fellow-travellers * * *
quid ni in curriculo vitæ. We are well come then so far, and
be the Almighty pleased to attend the remaining of your travel
with His protection and blessing. Grace be with you, and with
peace upon your family, and upon the land which you are serv-
ing so graciously.

"Also the same I wish heartily to your fellow laborers in the
ministry at Boston, to whom I present my respect, commending
my person and labors to their Godly remembrances.

" I have writ to his Honor Mr. Stoughton for to receive the
annual subvention assigned to me from the corporation of
which your honorable court hath assured the continuation in
my need. I shall not repeat here that your * * reverence hath
already heard from me, if I have any kind and comforting word
to expect from your reverence, I pray you direct it to the Rev.
Mr. Selyns, your worthy friend the minister of York. I remain
with a true and sincere respect of your reverence the most
humble and obliged servant

"DANIEL BONDET."

[*Addressed,* "*For the Reverend Master Increase Mather,
President of the College and Mr. of Divinity, Boston.*"] [1]

The delicacy and suavity of this letter are
marked, and it bespeaks a refinement which was
characteristic of the Huguenots. Its contrast in the
use of language with his representation to General
Court in 1691, before quoted, [2] is noticeable, and

---

[1] Mass. Arch., LVII. 59.   [2] Page 76.

shows his proficiency in the mastery of a strange
language.

Another letter, in which he gives us more information concerning himself than we get in any other
single document, is to Lord Cornbury, Governor of
New York.

[*D. Bondet to Lord Cornbury*, 1702.]

"MY LORD.

"I most humbly pray your Excellency to be pleased to
take cognizance of the petitioner's condition. I am a French
Refugee Minister, incorporated into the body of the Ministry
of the Anglican Church. I removed about fifteen years
ago into New England, with a company of poor refugees,
to whom lands were granted for their settlement, and to
provide for my subsistence I was allowed one hundred and five
pieces per annum, from the funds of the Corporation for the
Propagation of the Gospel among the Savages. I performed
that duty during nine years with a success approved and
attested by those who presided over the affairs of that Province.
The murders which the Indians committed in those countries
caused the dispersion of our company, some of whom fell by
the hands of the barbarians.

"I remained after that two years in that Province expecting
a favorable season for the re-establishment of affairs : but after
waiting two years seeing no appearance and being invited to
this Province of New York by Col. Heathcote who always
evinces an affection for the public good and distinguishes himself by a special application for the advancement of religion

and good order by the establishment of churches and schools, the fittest means to strengthen and encourage the people, I complied with his request, and that of the company of New Rochelle in this Province where I passed five years on a small allowance promised me by New Rochelle, of one hundred pieces and lodging, with that of one hundred and five pieces which the Corporation continued to me until the arrival of my Lord Bellomont, who, after indicating his willingness to take charge of me and my canton, ordered me thirty pieces in the Council of York, and did me the favor to promise me that, at his journey to Boston, he would procure me the continuation of that stipend that I had in times past. But having learned at Boston through M. Nanfan, his Lieutenant, that I annexed my signature to an ecclesiastical certificate which the churches and pastors of this Province had given to Sieur Delius minister of Albany, who had not the good fortune to please his late lordship, his defunct Excellency cut off his thirty pieces which he had ordered me in his Council at York, deprived me of the Boston pension of twenty-five pieces, writing to London to have that deduction approved and left me during three years last past in an extreme destitution of the means of subsistence.

"I believe, my Lord that in so important service as that in which I am employed, I ought not to discourage myself, and that the Providence of God which does not abandon those who have recourse to His aid by well doing, would provide in its time for my relief.

"Your Excellency's equity, the affection you have evinced to us for the encouragement of those who employ themselves constantly and faithfully in God's service, induce me to hope that I shall have a share in the dispensation of your justice, to relieve me from my suffering, so that I may be aided and

encouraged to continue my service in which by duty and gratitude I shall continue with my flock to pray God for the
preservation of your person, of your illustrious family, and the
prosperity of your government.

"Remaining your Excellency's humble and most respectful
servant

"DANIEL BONDET." [1]

This letter was favorably received, and through
the intercession of influential friends, his wants were
relieved, and he continued his labors with the church
at New Rochelle, with success, and died there in
1722, greatly lamented by his people.

His memory has been preserved among the people of Oxford, in the name of the beautiful meadow
in the southerly part of the town, which was owned
by him while living here. [2]

Another man of influence in the colony, was the
constable, Andrew Sigourney. This office, in those
days, was more important than it is in our country
towns at present. The constable was the right arm
of the law, and its only executive under the magistrate. He was also collector, and all public moneys
passed through his hands.

Sigourney was a man of mature age, being forty-

---

[1] Documentary Hist. State of New York, III. 929-931.
[2] Addenda B and H.

eight at the time of his coming to New Oxford.
Of his family, we learn that a daughter, Mrs. Johnson, and one son, (Andrew,) and probably two, were
here. [1] Mrs. James Butler, in her reminiscences
given to Dr. Holmes, says the Huguenots were in
Oxford eighteen or nineteen years. [2] This statement, from one of the family descendants, would
lead us to conclude that the Sigourneys were of the
second colony as well as the first. If so, they
evidently had a large interest in the place, and,
considering their sad experience in the first
attempt, showed strength of character and courage
in returning.

In the introduction to the "Genealogy of the
Sigourney family," by H. H. W. Sigourney, Prof.
J. D. Butler says : —

"Andrew Sigourney, the first of the name of whom we have
any record or knowledge, is said to have been comfortably
settled at or near Rochelle, in France, when the Edict of

---

[1] There are in New England other families of this name who
do not trace their descent to Andrew, son of the constable.
From this fact, and also from the tradition that other children
came from France with Andrew, senior, it is highly probable
that there were here with him, two sons, at least. — Sigourney
Genealogy.

[2] Holmes, 77.

Nantes was revoked, Oct. 22d, 1685. That report came to his knowledge when absent from home, to which he immediately hastened, and informed his wife that she must choose at once conformity to Papal Canons, or forsake all at a moment's warning; his determination he declared to be not to submit or bow to Baal. He found her ready to say, 'Thy God shall be my God.' Two suits of clothes were put upon each of their (four?) children, and the whole family, without preparation or attempt to secure their property — without even waiting to partake of the dinner which was preparing for them — hurried on board a friendly vessel, and were conveyed to England. Under the auspices of Gov. Dudley and others, proprietors of Oxford, Massachusetts, they were assisted to proceed to America, arriving at Fort Hill, in Boston, late in the autumn of 1686." [1]

Du Tuffeau, after the first breaking up, went to New Rochelle. We find his name in a list of inhabitants there in 1698, and his age given as fifty-two years. He seems to have been in good standing, as he was chosen the recorder of the town, and the first twenty-three pages of the records are of his writing. He resigned his office March 13, 1702, when the book was "found correct," and he was "discharged with thanks for his administration." [2]

---

[1] For account of Sigourney family, see Addenda M.
[2] Dr. Baird.

Bernon, in his petition to Gov. Shute, says of him :

" being through poverty obliged to abandon said plantation, [he] sold his cattle and other movables for his own particular use, went to London, and there died in a hospital."

He also states that he had at different times advanced money to Du Tuffeau, so that he now owed him more than one thousands pounds, which he counted as lost. He is styled "Gentleman" in the deed from Dudley and company, and also in the letter of administration on his estate.

Laborie, who went from Oxford to New York as successor to Rev. Pierre Peiret in 1704, continued his labors there until 1706, when he was discharged by the Consistory. [1]

The researches of Dr. Baird have brought to light the record of the will of Jean Martin, of New Rochelle, and formerly of New Oxford. It is dated " New Rochelle, Oct. 5th, 1700."

[Translation.]

"I Jean Martin, laborer, * * * declare that whereas it is the pure truth that my said wife and I having arrived in this place, New Rochelle, naked and having nothing but our arms

---

[1] Dr. Baird.

to gain our bread with, we have toiled in the sweat of our brows
to build and furnish the house we now live in and to clear and
enclose the lands pertaining thereunto. * * * Wherefore I
deem it right and reasonable and it is my will that when it shall
have pleased the Lord to withdraw me to Himself, my said wife
Anne Martin shall enter into full possession of all that belongs
to me, as well here as in the place of New Oxford, where we
formerly lived in New England."

This quaint and curious document gives some in-
sight into the character of Martin, and is interesting
in itself. But a greater interest attaches to it from
the fact that it shows us one who was typical of
most of the men who first settled New Oxford. In
their humble sphere they wrought and endured as
true men, to their own honor, the honor of God, and
of the religion they professed.

While we sympathize with them under their great
trials and misfortunes, their loyalty to the truth and
to each other, and their fortitude and constancy
under adversity, cannot fail to awaken our admira-
tion, and a regard which is almost a reverence,
for their memory.

CHAPTER XI.

Of the industries of the place the records give us
very little information. Here, as in all new places,
necessarily the first and chief business was subduing
and cultivating the land ; and it has been seen that
the aim of the settlers in coming here was to gain a
living chiefly from the soil. Yet it appears that the
active mind of Bernon was on the alert, to seize
every business opportunity which promised a profit-
able return. We have seen with what zeal he entered
upon the scheme for the manufacture of ship stores
from the forests here. We learn further, from his
papers, that he took up another more promising line
of manufacture, which was the making of glove or
wash leather from the deer skins which were
abundant then in this region, and which, when
dressed, were made use of by both the colonists and
natives, for a great variety of purposes. Associated
with him in this business were René Grignon and

Jean Papineau. The manufacture was carried on as late as 1704. [1]

According to the statement of Dea. Ebenezer Humphrey, there lived, about the commencement of the present century, near the "old mill place," a Frenchman named Bourdine or Bourdille, believed to have been of Huguenot stock, but it is not known that he left any descendants. [2] With this exception we have no evidence that any of the Huguenot

[1] One process in this manufacture, was beating the skins with heavy hammers in a mill. The mystery of the "wash leather mill" is here solved. The "chamoiserie," or tannery, contained some kind of apparatus similar to a fulling mill, used in the manufacture. The location of the tannery is not positively known, but the indications are that it was at the upper mill site.

"It is clear that Grignon was then living in Oxford. Deer-skins are mentioned in Bernon's accounts, in connection with the tannery."—[Dr. Baird.] In 1707, Grignon was with Bernon in Rhode Island. From the fact of his having been an Elder in the French Church, in Boston in 1700, and also from the manner in which he is referred to by Governor Dudley in the postscript of his letter to Bernon, —page 98, — we judge him to have been a man of considerable influence.

[2] We can account for the manner in which Dea. Humphrey spoke of this man, both to Andrew Sigourney and Dr. Holmes [Holmes, 80, 81] only on the supposition that he knew or believed him to be of Huguenot origin.

colonists returned to Oxford after its final desertion
in 1704. Some seventy-five or eighty years after
that time, two members of the Sigourney family, of
the fourth generation from Andrew Sigourney the
constable, came here and took up a permanent residence. The descendants of these two persons are
all of the Huguenot lineage known to be in Oxford
at the present time. [1]

It has been claimed by some historians that Peter
Shumway, who settled in Oxford in 1713, came to
America with Sigourney and others, and was one of
the original French settlers. This belief has been
entertained in the family, and, generally, among
Oxford people. But the testimony of the records is
against it. We find a petition of Peter Shumway of
Oxford, presented to the State authorities in 1750, in

---

[1] They are Mr. Archibald Campbell, his sons and grandchildren,
Mrs. A. W. Porter, Mr. Charles A. Sigourney and children and
grandchild, Mr. George W. Sigourney and daughter, the wife
and children of Rev. W. F. Lhoyd, Mr. George W. Sibley and
Mr. R. Nelson Sibley, with their children, and Mrs. Clara Wat-
son and daughter.

Hon. James B. Campbell, of Charleston, S. C.; Prof. James D.
Butler, Madison, Wis.; Peter Butler, Esq., of Boston; Colonel
J. W. Wetherell, of Worcester; Richard Olney, Esq., of Boston,
and Peter B. Olney, Esq., of New York, are of the same lineage.

9

which he says his father, Peter Shumway of Topsfield, was in the service of the country in the
Narragansett war, and was at the taking of the
Indian Fort, in 1675.[1] We find also, in the records,
that the Peter Shumway who came to Oxford in
1713 was born in Topsfield in 1678, so that he
was only eight years of age at the time of the
settlement. We have, by tradition, evidence which
cannot be discredited, that Peter the soldier came
from France. It becomes, then, a question of much
interest as to the origin of the present form of the
name. It carries in itself evidence that it is
not French, and search in the principal lists of
English surnames fails to identify it as English.
The direct conclusion is, that it is a corruption of a
French name. A clue to the settlement of the ·
question, seems to be given in the Essex county
records. Here—among the earliest entries it will
be observed — it is spelled "Shamway," which is
so nearly a correct expression in English of the
French name "Chamois," as to lead to the belief
that this was the original name. [2]

---

[1] For this petition, see Addenda P.

[2] An example of a similar change, of recent date, familiar to
the people of Oxford, is that of " Benoit " to " Benway."

On this point Dr. Baird writes as follows : —

"MY DEAR SIR :

"In view of the tradition regarding the French extraction of the Shumway family, I can only offer the conjecture that the name may have undergone a transformation similar to that which has befallen many Huguenot names in England and America. *If French*, the name 'Chamois'[1] offers a probable solution. The transition from this to 'Shumway' would be very easy. A Protestant family bearing this name is mentioned in a list of fugitives from the neighborhood of Saint Maixent, in the old province of Poitou, (in the present department of Deux-Sèvres,) France, at the period of the Revocation of the Edict of Nantes. A number of Huguenots found their way to New England at an earlier day : and a Chamois, the founder of the Shumway family, may have been one of these.

"Very truly yours,

"CHARLES W. BAIRD.[2]

"GEORGE F. DANIELS, Esq."

The existing relics of the colony are few. We learn from people now living, that seventy-five years ago, near the sites of the dwellings, which were easily traced by the cellars, many apple trees of large-

---

[1] Pronounced *Shamwah*.

[2] For extracts from Essex county and Topsfield records, and other matters relating to the subject, see Addenda Q.

growth and apparently of great age, existed, and within fifty years past, decaying remains of orchards were standing in positions that indicated that they were set by the hands of the Huguenots. [1] In the record of the doings of the selectmen of Oxford, we find that in February, 1714, the year after the settlement by the English, a road was laid out from the "eight-rod road," easterly, near the "old mill place," "on the south side of an orchard." [2] That orchard is well remembered by persons now living, and was directly between the old mill site and the main street.

The locations of the larger portion of the Huguenot houses could be traced, forty years ago, by the hollows in the earth, but to-day very few of them can be found.

Fortunately we have one memento worthy of preservation, which by tradition has been marked for many years as genuine — the chimney stone of the Johnson house. This is a straight, smooth, unhammered stone about six feet long, sixteen to eighteen

---

[1] Addenda E. and G.   [2] Addenda G.

[3] A few years since, Mr. E. D. Rich filled two of these hollows which were near the upper mill site, and which probably marked the location of the dwellings of those who had care of the mills.

inches wide, and six inches thick. It may now be seen near the entrance of Memorial Hall.

The best known relic is the ruin of the large fort. This place was examined by Dr. Holmes and Prof. Brazer in 1819, when they "traced the lines of the bastions of the fort." [1]

In 1846, Mr. Allen, before named, visited it, made some measurements, and projected a plan of it which was published in the "History of Narragansett Church," page 61. He says "sufficient, however, remain of the foundation stones and of portions of the walls of a salient angle, to indicate to the eye of a visitor the military design of the only remaining fortification of masonry that still serves to perpetuate recollections of the bloody scenes of the Indian wars among the now peaceful hills of New England."

Many years ago the walls of the structure were removed, down to the foundation stones, excepting on the south line, where parts of the original wall may be seen, but which is mainly a confused mass three or four feet high, overgrown with wild grape vines and bushes, among which may be seen cinnamon roses, currants, and asparagus, believed to be relics of the garden which flourished in the vicinity at the time of the occupation.

---

[1] Holmes, 80.

No change, other than that which time inevitably brings, has been made in these remains for the last fifty years. The outline of the southern wall indicates that a small portion of it at the southwestern angle projected a few feet, and formed what might have answered the end of a "salient angle." But no signs of bastions are now to be seen. So far as can be judged by its present appearance, it was little more than a strong enclosure, built without mortar, of the rough surface stones, and perhaps, in parts, of timber. Its dimensions were about seventy-five by one hundred and five feet, and the foundation indicates a wall from four to five feet in thickness. The southern wall extended westerly beyond the corner, about forty feet; apparently as a cover to the entrance at the southwestern angle. John Mayo, aged eighty-one, who lived near the place, said "there was a very considerable house, with a cellar, well, etc., within it." [1] The place of the well is now distinctly marked.

This does not appear to have been in any sense a public work, but was built at Bernon's expense, and was under his control, as a necessity to his interests as well as those of the colonists. As he does not mention it when making specifications to Gov. Shute,

---

[1] Mrs. Lee, II. 64.

in his application for reimbursement, we conclude that it was a work of comparatively small cost.[1]

Mrs. Lee, quoting from the manuscript of John Mayo, says : " There was a garden outside the fort, on the west, containing asparagus, grapes, plums, cherries, and gooseberries. There were more than ten acres cultivated around the fort." Such a garden in the wilderness, when we consider circumstances, seems a strange thing, but doubtless a refined taste, and the desire to perpetuate in this new Western home some of the sweet memories of sunny France had much to do with its existence.

Mrs. L. H. Sigourney, in speaking of the plants growing on the ruined wall, says: " They were living tokens of the loved clime whence they were exiled." She adds :—

" Peculiar sacredness adheres to this spot. Hither they turned with their wives and little ones for a refuge, in a strange land. When the dread of a savage foe fell upon them, it was hallowed by their prayers to the God of all power and might."[2]

The most complete memento of the extinct colony is at the site of the upper mill, one mile easterly

---

[1] In the title of his plan of the fort, Mr. Allen says, " Built by Gabriel Bernon."

[2] Manuscript, December 20th, 1860.

from the main street. This relic has not been mentioned by any writer on the Oxford Huguenots, and is but little known in comparison with the other historic places. It is in the midst of a small meadow which is skirted by wooded uplands, and in midsummer is so overhung and shut in by trees and wild undergrowth as to be hidden from the casual observer. Here the substantial dam, some sixty feet in length, both wall and embankment, stands almost entire, — a deep trench to convey the water from the pond to the mill-wheel, a distance of seventy-five feet, is distinctly to be seen — the position of the mill can be fixed — and the wasteway, running from the wheel about one hundred feet to the stream below, seems to have been but recently made, so little has it been obstructed.

In this retired spot, the kindly hand of nature has protected and preserved the handiwork of the Huguenots, as it has been kept in no other locality in Oxford. The place is full of interest to the antiquary, and is well worth a visit, not only for its associations, but for its quiet, picturesque beauty.

The names of the Huguenot families who settled
New Oxford, so far as ascertained, are as follows :

1. —— Montel,	1. Ober Germon,
1. J. Dupeu,	1. Jean Maillet,
1. Capt. Jermon,	1. André Segourné,
1. Peter Canté,	1. Jean Millet on, *
1. Bureau l'aine,	1. Peter Canton,
1. Elie Dupeu,	4. I. Bertrand Du Tuffeau,
2. Jean Martin,	5. M. Alard,
3. M. Bourdille,	6. René Grignon.

In addition to these, Barber gives, p. 593 His. Col.:

M. Germaine,	M. Boudinot,
Jean Baudoin,	Benj. Faneuil.

Mr. Olney in his Address gives:

Paix Cazeneau, and "perhaps" Jean Beaudoin and Benjamin
Faneuil.

---

1 These signed Bernon's certificate, declaring themselves to
have been inhabitants of New Oxford. 2 Extract of whose
will we give. 3 Spoken of by Dea. Humphrey to Dr. Holmes,
4 Bernon's agent. 5 Children taken away by Indians. 6 In
"chamoiserie" in 1704.

* i. e., Jean Millet, or Maillet, anc. [ancien. Elder.] It
seems there were two of the name, perhaps father and son, and
the one was an Elder in the French Church.

On April 12, 1712, the original proprietors issued
the following :

[From a copy of the original in the Town Clerk's Office.]

PROCLAMATION.

———————

" We the under written with other owners and proprietors of
the lands at Oxford in the neepmug.country granted to us by
the general assembly of the Massachusetts colony, and since
otherwise ratified and confirmed to ourselves in the Kingdom
of Great Britain, having long time determined and surveyed
ten or twelve thousand acres for a village and settlement of
inhabitants and accordingly established a number of Frentch
Famalyes, Refugees, who have since deserted the place whereby
all improvements are lost which is a detriment to the province
as well as to ourselves in the hope of our own private advantage, by our other lands — do hereby agree and offer to thirty
English families that shall settle there to give grant and confirm
to them all the lands of the said village containing the said ten
thousand acres, except what is already granted to Mr. Bernon
which is ——— acres, to be laid out to them, first a quantity of
it in house lots not exceeding forty acres a family, and after the
rest in proper divisions as they may agree among themselves
always provided they be thirty families, and in the meantime if
ten families or more shall proceed forthwith within a year to
settle there, they shall have their house lots set out to them,
and they as they have the use of the other land meadows until the
number be thirty, and then they have liberty to divide the whole.

If any of the French families choose to come thither we do hereby save to ourselves liberty to establish them with other inhabitants, and Capt. Chandler the surveyor is hereby allowed to lay out lots accordingly, taking care always that he do not intrench upon the land of the proprietors.   .

Signed   J. DUDLEY,

WILLIAM TAYLOR,   ⎫
PETER SARGENT,   ⎪ Heirs and Exec-
——— SARGENT,   ⎬   utors of
JOHN DANFORTH,   ⎪ Wm. Stoughton.
ELIZA DANFORTH,   ⎭

In May, 1713, the surveying of house lots to those who had made choice of them with a view to settlement, began. By July the requisite number was complete, and on the eighth day of that month a deed from the proprietors to the thirty English colonists was executed, conveying to them the plat called the Village.

Thus commenced the permanent settlement of Oxford.

Upon the first page of the earliest existing records of Oxford there stands alone a word of deep signifi- cance, placed there by one of the fathers of the town, as a charge to the coming generations. That sug- gestive word may fitly close this imperfect recital of the experiences of

THE HUGUENOTS IN THE NIPMUCK COUNTRY.

Remember

ADDENDA.

WE learn from the Oxford records, that there were here when the English settlement began, improvements, [A.] orchards [E. and G.] and in one case a building [A.] left by the Huguenots — which were valuable, and for which those who came into possession of them were required to pay the Village Corporation. It appears that each man in the settlement chose his forty acres for a home lot wherever he saw fit, and the balance of the lands was divided by lot.

Joseph Chamberlin's choice of a house lot is the first recorded, and it may be presumed that, at least in his estimation, it was the best. [A.]

A. .

Pages 68, 108.

"may 13th, 1713. Surveyed for Joseph Chamberlin sen[r] Round the great house 40 acres being a home lott in oxford: and four acres and one Rood in it being allowed for a highway going through. * * * surveyed by John Chandler Jun. Approved and Established by order of the original proprietors provided he pay for the bettering his lott by former Improvement and building.

"By John Chandler, who made such an agreement at the beginning."—Village Rec. 13.

"Oxford the 4 of february 1714 Joseph Chambbarline siner House loute bein upoun boundet hel so caled, bounded on the nourest with a stake and a hape of stons rouneing a hundred and twenty rodes sovurly on burnnun line to a black oke running westerly sixty rods to a stack and a hepe of stones than rouning nurarly on hundred rods to a stack an Hepe stones foust named * * * provided he pays as tow men shal judge is beater than other lots in sd village."—Ibid. 2.

The highway which ran through this lot, was Woodstock "great trail," which ran from Johnson's plain, northeasterly over Bondet hill, and near the "great house," which stood on its eastern slope. A large hollow in the earth now marks the place of a building which Mr. John Mayo who was born and lived to old age, near the place, said was kept as a tavern, early in the town history. Whether it was the "great house" is a matter of conjecture. There is much room for speculation as to what this building was. Its being called a house would indicate that it was a dwelling, and if so, it probably was that of Bondet.

B.

Pages 51, 122.

"It was voted * * * in Nov. 30, 1714 that the committy

shall begin to lay out meddow att East End of the great meddow, from thence to the meddow on Ellat's mill brook, from
thence to the croth of the Reveir so down strame the Reveir:
to the line from thence to bundit's meddow."—Ibid. 4.

The fact that the committee were directed to pass the
Village line into Dudley's land, and go on to the "crotch"
of the river, etc., shows that on some conditions, he had
released to the Village a portion of his meadows, perhaps
to make up for the deficiency in the Bernon grant.

C.

Pages 70, 83.

"A way laid out by the selectmen beginning att a white oake
tree on Jonson's plain near Woodstock path running northwardly marked on the west sid to neland's feald on the great
plain by the old mill place, from thence marked on the East sid
by staks and trees tel it coms to the brooke on the Northwardly
sid of peter Shumway's frame of his house, from thence on the
West sid of the swamp to and by the ends of the houselots of
John town and Israel town and Daniel Eloit Juner sd way being
Eight rods wide laid out febeuary the sixt 1713–4."—Ibid. 1.

This "way" included the present Main street.

D.

Page 102.

Jan. 25th, 1714. "Voted at a lofel town meten that Danel
Elaet shauld buld a greust mel for the town yuse."—Ibid.

E.

Page 69.

Jan. 25th, 1714. "Voted that Ebbenzar Humphry should have the orchard Joyning to the Southwest corner of his home lot making allounce to the Town in money to full of what tow men shall judge it to be worth."—Ibid.

F.

Page 69.

"A way laid out from the four rod way to benieman nelands home lot, begining att a wihite oake tree on the lowlands on ye Southwardly Side of the frinch burying place, from thence marked on the North sid to nelands home lot, said way is tow rods wide. febeuary the sixt on 1713-4."—Ibid.

The conformation of the land on the southerly side of the reputed location of this burying place, agrees with this description.

G.

Page 132.

"a highway laid out by the Select men beginning att the Eight rod way on the southwardly sid of an orchard neer the old mill running over the old mill brook to a rock on the East of said Brooke, from thence marked on the northwardly side with mark trees tel it coms to barnon's land neer the North East corner of Joseph Chamberlin seneor's home lot said way being four rods wide." Feb. 6th, 1714.—Ibid.

This was the road from the main street to the fort.

H.

Page 122.

In the description of Nathaniel Chamberlin's lot, "Bundet" meadow is referred to.—Ibid. 48.

I.

Page 111.

Apr. 11th. 1721. The report of the committee of the Proprietors, chosen to act with Thomas Mayo, Joseph Weld and Samuel Davis, to settle the lines of the Bernon land, gives the following description : —

"begins at a heap of stones on a cleeft of Rock westward of a certain meadow commonly called the great meadow and from said heap of stones to extend N. one degree ten minutes E. 140 perch to a heap of stons, thence E. at right angles, 100 perch to a heap of stons, from thence northwardly at right Angles 112 perch to a heap of stons, thence Easterly at right angles 252 perch to a heap of stones [Oxford line,] thence southerly [on said town line] at right angles 280 perch to a heap of stons, thence S. 15° east 674 perch [on said Oxford line] to a heap of stones [Manchaug corner] thence westerly at right angles 474 perch to a heap of stons, thence Northerly at right angles 120 perch to a heap of stones, thence W. 4° N. 154 perch to a heap of stons, thence N. 13° E. 464 perch to a black oak tree, thence Northerly 56 perch to a heap of stones, thence E. 6° S. 104 perch to a heap of stones, thence N. 12° E. 120 perch to a heap of stons, thence W. 12° N. 148 perch to the heap of stons first mentioned."—Ibid. 16.

10

Sept. 21st, 1721. "Y⁰ quistion was put whether yᵉ return of yᵉ committe chosen Mar. 27th 1721 to settel and make bounds between the proprietors and those who bought Mr. Bernon's Farm as it was set forth by the plat and wrighting which was voted in the affirmative."—Ibid. 44.

J.

Page 107.

The following votes show that the town conceded Bernon's rights in the deeded land : —

"Att a lawfull town meeting held in Oxford Oct. 15 1714 it was aggreed upon and voted that the 172 acars of meddow which is to be taken out of gabrel barnons farm shall be taken up at the great meddow."

"was voted at the same meeting that Nathaniel Chamberlin's lot should be layed to the land taken up in barnons farm for want of a mesuer of meddow which we were to take in one piece if it can be done."—Ibid.

There were not, "in one piece," 172 acres of meadow in Bernon's tract. The dotted line on the map shows what was taken from the "farm" at the great meadow.

Bernon was taxed, Sept. 4, 1717, for the support of the gospel in Oxford. His name is first on the list, and the amount is larger than that of any other landholder.

An entry occurs as follows : —

"Sept. 12 1720. Voted and chose Ebenezer Learned and

ĭ

Isaac Larned to act in our behalf in making demand of what is
due from Mr. Bernon to us according to his deed or lease, and
receive the same."

We know of no reasonable explanation of this vote,
except the supposition that Dudley and Company had
made over to the village their claim of the annual quit
rent due from Bernon.

K.

Page 75.

This deed in substance is as follows : —

" This indenture made the 24th day of May A. D. 1688
*   *   *   between Joseph Dudley of Roxbury, William
Stoughton of Dorchester *   *   * Esqs. Robert Thompson
of London *   *   * Merchant, Daniel Cox of London aforesaid, Doctor in Physick, and John Blackwell of Boston *   *   *
Esq. on the one part and Gabriel Bernon of Boston aforesaid,
Merchant on the other part—Witnesseth

" Whereas Isaac Barton, [Bertrand,] Gentleman, hath heretofore had the allowance [of said parties of the first part] to elect
and make choice of 500 acres of land *   *   * within *   *   *
the southeast angle of [a tract of land called New Oxford
village] to and for the use of him the said Barton and the said
Gabriel Bernon, *   *   * and whereas since the electing of
the said 500 acres, he [Bertrand] hath proposed that he may
have 250 acres more of said land *   *   * to the use aforesaid; and he the said Gabriel Bernon that he may have 1750

acres more of the said lands. * * * adjoining to the said
500 acres to and for the use of said Gabriel Bernon, his heirs
and assigns —

"Now these presents witness that [the above named parties
of the first part] as well for and in consideration that the said
Gabriel Bernon hath undertaken and by these presents doth
undertake and engage within twelve months after the day of the
date of these presents at his own proper cost and charges to
erect build and maintain a Corn or Grist Mill in some convenient and fitting place within the said town of Oxford for the use
of the Inhabitants of said town and village [unto which mill
* * * said inhabitants shall be obliged] at all times forever
hereafter to make their suit as also for and in consideration of
the sum of 5 shillings * * * paid by said Bernon * * *
and the rents and covenants hereafter mentioned * * *
[the parties of the first part] do grant bargain sell and confirm
to the said Isaac Barton and Gabriel Bernon * * * all that
tract * * * of 500 acres * * * elected as aforesaid
by said Isaac Barton, to hold to them the said Isaac Barton and
Gabriel Bernon * * * and all that and those 250 acres
more desired by said * * * Barton as aforesaid, and 1750
acres more desired by the said Gabriel Bernon adjoining to the
said 500 acres * * * within the southeast angle of Oxford
village * * * as followeth * * *

"Beginning at a walnut tree marked (S. D.) standing at the
west angle of Manchaug—and thence running W. 15° S. 352
perches, and from thence to be set off by a line to be drawn
parallel to the utmost easterly line and bounds of the said
Oxford village * * * as far as will complete the full
quantity of 2872 acres * * * so that if the said line shall
not extend unto and include and take in the utmost westerly

part of the said 500 acres * * * said Barton elected for
himself and the said Gabriel Bernon * * * the said 500
acres shall nevertheless be included * * * within the
* * * 2872 acres aforementioned * * * the whole
quantity of 2872 acres shall be set out accordingly whereof the
forementioned 500 acres and 250 acres more desired by the said
Isaac Barton to be jointly held and enjoyed by them the said
Isaac Barton and Gabriel Bernon * * * also 1750 acres
more thereof to be held and enjoyed by him the said Gabriel
Bernon [his heirs and assigns for their use and behoof] and 200
acres more thereof to the use of Daniel Bondet, his heirs and
assigns forever.

"Excepting and reserving to [said parties of the first part] 172
acres of meadow land * * * in one entire parcel and
adjoining unto the lands of Manchaug aforesaid [in such place
as they may choose.]

"And providing [the parties of the first part or any two or
more of them resident in New England may lay out over such
lands] such common paths or ways * * * as they shall
judge necessary or commodious for the said [township or village.] Yielding and paying therefor yearly and every year on
the 24th of March at or in the Town house of Boston aforesaid, unto [said parties of the first part] or to their certain
attorney deputy or agent by them * * * appointed to
receive the same. the annual rent of 40 shillings current money
of New England. * * * And the said Gabriel Bernon for
himself his heirs and assigns * * * doth covenant grant
and agree with [the parties of the first part] that he [or his
heirs or assigns] will well and truly pay or cause to be paid to
the said [parties of the first part] the said yearly rent [as afore-

said] and that in case of non-payment thereof or any part
thereof [it shall be lawful for the parties of the first part to]
enter said premises and distrain and the distresses there found
from time to time to lead carry away sell or dispose at such
rates as they can get for the same * * * and with the
proceeds imburse and satisfy themselves [for all arrearages and
charges] rendering the overplus (if any be) to him the said
Gabriel Bernon * * *

"And that in case of his the said Isaac Barton and Gabriel
Bernon deserting or relinquishing the said lands [or there shall
not be found on said premises sufficient goods] for satisfying
within any twelve months after the same shall grow due, this
present grant and all the matters and things therein contained
shall thenceforth cease, determine, and be utterly null and void,
and the lands * * * shall revert * * * unto [the said
parties of the first part] and shall and may lawfully be by them
entered upon, possessed and enjoyed as in their former
estate * * *

"[The parties of the first part] covenant and agree with said
Isaac Bartron and Gabriel Bernon their heirs and assigns [that
they the said Bartron and Bernon performing the afore named
acts faithfully as specified, may] have hold and enjoy the
premises hereby granted against [said parties of the first part]
or any other person or persons lawfully claiming or to claim the
same or any part thereof * * * by, from or under them or
any of them.

"In witness whereof the said Joseph Dudley, William
Stoughton, Robert Thompson, Daniel Cox and John Blackwell
have hereunto set their hands and seals the day and year first
above written. JOSEPH DUDLEY and a seal, WILLIAM

STOUGHTON and a seal, JOHN BLACKWELL and a seal.   Feb. 6th 1690 William Stoughton Esq. and John Blackwell Esq. acknowledge this Instrument to be their voluntary act and deed. Before SAM^L SEWALL Ass'it.

"Signed sealed and delivered in presence of us by Joseph Dudley, William Stoughton and John Blackwell. DANIEL ALLEN, RICHARD WILKINS, JNO. HERBERT HOWARD, Suffolk &c.   Boston 5th of February 1716.   The Hon. Joseph Dudley Esq. personally appeared before me the Subscriber one of His Majesty's Justices of the Peace in Said County, and did acknowledge this Instrument to be his free act and deed — SAMUEL LYNDE — February 5th, 1716.

"Received and accordingly entered and examined.

"JOHN BALLANTYNE Reg^r ."

—Suffolk Co. Rec., XXX. 268.

L.

Page 76.

["*contract De Mr Cherch pour Le Moulin de New-oxford.*"]

"Articles of Agreement had made concluded and agreed upon by and Between Caleb Church of Watertown Millright and Gabriel Bernon of Boston Merc^t this   Day of March Anno Domini One Thousand six hundred Eight Eight Nine.

"Imp^s   The said Caleb Church doth Covenant and Agree with the s^d Gabriel Bernon that he shall and vill att his own Proper Costs and Charges Erect Build and ffinish a Corn or

Grist mill in all Poynts workemanlike in Such Place in the
Village of Oxford as shall by the s^d Bernon be Directed the
s^d Mill House to be Twenty two foot Long and Eighteen foot
Broad and Eleven foot stud Substantially and Sufficiently
covered with a Jett to Cover the Wheele and a Chamber fitt for
the Laying and Disposing Corn Bags or other Utensills
Necessary for the s^d Mill and the s^d Church doth Covenant to
find att his Own Proper Costs all the Iron Worke Necessary
for the s^d Mill and all other Things Except what is hereafter
Expressed

"Item, The said Gabriel Bernon doth Covenant and Agree
with the said Caleb Church that hee will bee att the Charge of
searhing Preparing and Bringing to Place the Mill Stones for
the s^d mill and that he will by the Oversight and Direction of
the s^d Church Make Erect and finish the Earth of the Dame
that shall bee by the s^d Church adjudged necessary for the
s^d Mill and also will dig and Prepare the Place where the Mill
shall be Erected and also will allow to the s^d Church five
hundred foot of Boards and   Persons to help for the Cutting
Down of the Timber and will bee att the Charge of Bringing
the Timber to Place and further doth Covenant to Pay to the
s^d Church for his Labor and Pains herein the Sume of forty
Pounds two thirds thereof in money the Other Third in goods
att money price in Three Equall Payments One Third att the
ffalling the Timber One Third att the Raising and the Last att
the finishing the s^d mill

"Lastly The s^d Church doth Covenant and Promies to finish
the s^d Mill all sufficient and workemanlike and Sett her to

Worke by the Last day of Augt next after the Day of the Date
hereof In Wittness whereof they have hereunto sett their
hands and seals the day and Year first above written

                          "CALEB CHURCH.   [*Seal.*]
"Sealed and Delivered
"in Presence of

"I. BERTRAND DUTUFFEAU
"THO DUDLEY."

Endorsed on the back of the original paper is the
following:

"Within named Caleb Church do ingage and promis to find
the stones and laye them on to make mele at my one costs and
charge for the which Mr Bernon doth ingage and promis to
paye for the same one and twenty pounds in corent mony for
the same to be concluded when the mile grinds

"Boston May: ye 20: 1689
   "RICHARD WILKINS   CALEB CHURCH
   "EDMOND BROWNE   GABRIEL BERNON."
                                          [*Seal.*]

Next follows this statement:

                                          £   s: d
"ffor the mill in first the sum of forty pounds   40: 00:
secondly for the stones of the said one and
    twenty pounds   21: 00:
forthely for an addition to the house six pounds   6: 00:
(sic)   ─────────
                                                   67: 00:"

Then follow two receipts from Mr. Church :

"Received one third Part of the within mentioned sume of forty wch is Thirteen Pounds six shillings and Eight Pence two thirds in money and one third in Goods by me

"Caleb Church."

"More I have received fifty three pounds tirteen shillings wich the above said sum are in all the sum of sixty and seven pounds in full following our s^d bargain Boston : 4 february 1689–90 received by my

"Caleb Church."

"Peter Basset   in witness

"Gabriel Depont   present."

— Bernon Papers. — Dr. Baird.

M.

Page 124.

Andrew Sigourney, the constable, died in Boston, April 16th, 1727, aged eighty-nine years, and was interred in the Granary burial ground, near the grave of Pierre Daillè. His children were — Andrew, born in France in 1673, and Susan, also born in France, who married, first, John Johnson, who was killed by the Indians, and, second,

Daniel Johonnot, her cousin, of Boston. Andrew married Mary Germaine, who was born in France, 1680. He was a distiller, and one of the proprietors of the French church, and executed, with others, a deed conveying it, May 7th, 1748. He died in 1748. Andrew and Mary Germaine Sigourney had nine children, the fifth being Anthony, who married, first, Mary Waters of Salem, and, second, Elizabeth Breed, m. n. Whittemore. Anthony and Mary Waters Sigourney had three children, the first being Mary, who married James Butler. They came to Oxford to live soon after the revolutionary war, and from them descended the Butler and Campbell families, well known for fifty years past in Oxford. Anthony and Elizabeth Breed Sigourney had two children the second being Andrew, born Nov. 30th, 1752. He married, July 26th, 1787, Elizabeth Wolcott, daughter of Josiah Wolcott, Esq., and granddaughter of Rev. John Campbell, the first English minister of Oxford. From them descended all of the name since living in the town. " He was apprenticed to a sail maker in Boston, went to Newfoundland and worked at his trade till the revolutionary war broke out, and came then to his uncle Holman (?) in Sutton, Mass. He, with his brother Anthony, and cousin (?) Jonathan Holman, entered the army * * * were in the battle at White Plains and other engagements. He obtained a commission as commissary, with the rank of Captain. In 1784 he settled in

Oxford, and became wealthy in trade." — [Sigourney Genealogy.] He commenced business with Mr. Butler, the husband of his half sister, and continued with him about ten years. Their store was at the place known as the " Butler tavern," near the old common. About 1794 he removed to the centre of the town, and was in trade alone until about 1825, when he gave up his business to his eldest son, William.

N.

Page 92.

As illustrative of the Indian character, we give two incidents which occurred in the early history of Oxford, which come to us well authenticated.

A town meeting was assembled on a certain day at the old tavern on the Plain, which stood at the corner where the Post Office now is. In that meeting was a party of noisy, drunken Indians, who became so annoying that the moderator called upon Col. Ebenezer Learned, one of the first English settlers, — a courageous and powerful man, — to have them removed. Learned approached the ringleader, and, stooping, placed his head between the legs of the intruder, and raising him up, lifted him upon his shoulders. Then calling upon the rest of the company to follow, he marched across the hall, down the stairs, and out into the middle of the street, where he deposited his burden in a sitting posture, and there left him.

A few days afterward, as he was at work in his sawmill at the "upper falls" — now the site of the "Huguenot Mill" at North Oxford — looking westward into the woods, he saw a large number of Indians filing down the hillside toward the mill. As they approached the open ground, he took his gun in hand and walked out to reconnoitre. Upon seeing him they at once laid down their guns and other weapons, and came towards him in a friendly manner, and after saluting him, asked him to stand still a little while, as they had something to give him. They then returned to the woods, and soon re-appeared, bringing with them a quantity — an armful, as the story goes — of valuable furs, which they presented to him as a token of their gratitude for his considerate and kind treatment of the drunken members of their tribe who had disturbed the late town meeting.

The other incident relates to an experience of Learned in his own house at North Oxford.

At candle light one cold evening, an Indian came to his door and asked for food and shelter. He was kindly received, and after supper was allowed to camp before the large open fire-place in the old-fashioned kitchen. Some time during the night the Colonel became conscious of a presence stooping over him as he lay in bed. The Indian, perceiving that he was awake, said to him in a scornful tone, "You, pale face!" Learned was out of bed in an instant, and with a well-directed blow laid the fellow upon the floor, and in a few seconds had him outside the house and the door shut upon him.

He saw no more of his visitor for about a year, when he again made his appearance, at evening, as before. He had in his hand a roll of valuable furs, which he presented respectfully to Learned, with the laconic remark, " *You brave*," and left without ceremony.

O.

Page 98.

[Agreement between Gabriel Bernon and Oliver and Nathanael Coller.]

" Know all men by these presents that I Gabril Bernon hath bargind with and let vnto Oluer Coller and Nathanel Coller my howse and farme at new oxford Called the olde mill; with four Cowes and Calfes the which said farm and Cowes I have let for five years upon the Conditions as foloweth —— that they brake up and monnure and plant with orchod two Acers and half of land with in the s^d Term of Fiue and also to spend the remain-part of their time to work upon the other lands ; and all that is soed dow now to ly to English grass and at the end of fiue years for s^d oluer Coller and Nathanel Coller for them to resine up peceble posestion of the s^d hous farm and four Cowes and Calves and half the increes to the s^d Gabril Bernon or his heirs or asigns the s^d two Acers and half of land ly a boue the spring on the side of the hill; and for thare in Courigment I haue let them one pare of oxen for one year, the which s^d oxen they must Deliuer to me at s^d term ; and in case the oxen be lost they must make them good ; Exsept by the enemy.

" to the performence of this our bargin we have heer unto set
our hands in the presents of us ——

memerandom they have
ingaged to brak up half
one Acer of land evere
year and to pay the three
first yers six shilling p year
and two last years to
pay tweny shilling p   " The mark of X OLUER COLLER
year and we have   " The mark of — NATHANAEL COLLER
ualled the s^d four
Cows at tw pounds

      " JOSEPH TWICHELS
      " THOMAS ALLERTON "

P.

Page 130.

" TO THE HONORABLE SPENCER PHIPS ESQ LIEUT GOV-
ERNOR AND COMMANDER IN CHIEF IN AND OVER HIS
MAJESTIE'S PROVINCE OF THE MASSACHUSETTS BAY
IN NEW ENGLAND: THE HONORABLE COUNCIL AND
HOUSE OF REPRESENTATIVES IN GENERAL COURT
ASSEMBLED :

" The Memorial of Peter Shumway of Oxford most humbly
sheweth that whereas your humble memorialist did many years
ago prefer a petition to the Honorable General Court of this
Province praying that as he is the legal heir and representative
of Peter Shumway of Topsfield who was a long time in the

service of this Country and particularly in the Narragansett war, and taking the Indian fort there which he in said petition proved by living testimonies and which he believes the Honorable John Chandler and others worthy members of this Honorable Court do yet remember,

"And whereas your aged, decrepid and poor memorialist hath never yet received any gratuity, or reward in land or otherwise for his said father's services and sufferings as many others have done, your most humble memorialist again most humbly prayeth this Honorable Court in their wonted goodness and compassion would make him a grant of some piece of Country land for said services, or otherwise as in their great wisdom they [see] fit: which will oblige your most humble memorialist — as in duty bound will ever pray.

"(Signed)   PETER SHUMWAY.
"March 23, 1749-50."
                                          — Mass. Arch., XLVI. 212.

This paper is in the handwriting of Rev. John Campbell, Minister of Oxford from 1721 to 1761.

Q.

Page 131.

[Extracts from the Records of Essex County.]

BIRTHS IN TOPSFIELD.

" Peeter sonn of Peeter Shumway borne the 6th of June 1678.
"John, son of Peter Shamway borne the 20th January 1679-80.

"Samuell Shamway son of Peeter Shamway borne 2th November 1681.

"The birth of Dorcas Shumway daughter of Peter and Francis Shumway y⁰ 16 Oct 1683.

"Joseph son to Peter and Francis Shumway Octo. 13, 1686."

[*From Topsfield Town Records.*]

"Peter Shumway and Mariah Smith both of Boxford¹ ware married on y⁰ 11th day of February 1700-1."

["She was daughter of Robert and Mary, B. 1677, Dec. 18."]

—Letter of John H. Gould.—Topsfield.

[*From Congregational Church Records, Topsfield.*]

"Valentine Butler and Dorcas Shumway married 1711 November 26."

BAPTISMS.

"Peter Shumway, his

"Oliver — May 10, 1702.   Jeremiah — Mar. 21, 1703.

"David — Dec. 23, 1705.   Mary — May 9, 1708.

"Samuel — April 22, 1711.   John — Aug. 15, 1713."

[These children, if living, probably came to Oxford with

¹ Boxford joins Topsfield on the west, and while they lived in Boxford they still continued their connection with the Topsfield church.

11

their parents in 1713. Three others — Jacob, Hepzibah, and Amos — were born in Oxford.]

[Extract from a "Book of Accounts" of John Gould, Topsfield, selected from twenty-four entries of accounts with "Goodwife Shomway,¹ from 1699 to 1708.]

"Goodwife Shomway Crd Six days of John and one day of Samuell to thrash, and a pair of oxen one day.

"The 29 november 1699 goodwife Shomway   Dr
"to weaving fortty three yeards of cloth at 4d yᵉ yeard money,   14—4

"Reconed with Goodwife Shomway the Sixt day of July 1700 and there Rest dew to me the sum of Sixteen Shillings and four pence in money in another place.   0—12—6

"Goodwife Shomway Dr. to weaving a peas of yd. wide cloth sometime in the begingin of the winter 1702 and I have forgot how much it was. I have found it in another place to be 33 yeards at 4d the yard three yeards of it was striped at 6d. the yeard.

"July the 23 1705 paid to goodwife Shumway 16 shillings there is 12 shillings due to her in this Reconing of money that I had for her cloth and I had 3 quarters of a pound of linnin yearn of her to strick my slay Credit is of Linsywoolsi cloth one year[d] & half.

---

¹ Evidently the wife of Peter, the Soldier.

"Goodwife Shomway Cr't to half a bushel of wheat   2s 6d one peck of beans o—1—o one pound and a half of flax   1—2 to twelve shillins for Intrast money.

"October 12 1708. Cozen Shomway Credit to 87 pounds of beefe at 2d per pound   o—14—6

"November 1708. Cozen Shomway Dr. to weaving 29 yerds cloth   14—6

"Reconed with Goodwife Shomway the 23d day of desember 1807 in two other places in this book and there is that pease yt mary wove I hant found how much it was yet but all other Reconings cleared to this day and I owe her 16 shillings and six pence the pease that mary wove above sd was thirty-seven yeards 4 d. the yeard."

INDEX.